Spiritual Warfare

How to Enforce Your God-Given Supernatural Authority
TO NEUTRALISE DEMONIC ACTIVITY, OVERCOME DEMONIC STRATEGIES
AND PULL DOWN STRONGHOLDS

AN EXPOSÉ *of* SATAN'S LIES *and* TRICKERY

By Uebert Angel

LEVI HOUSE PUBLICATIONS

Unless otherwise stated, all scripture quotations are taken from the King James Version of the Bible.

ISBN 978-0-9957499-6-2

Copyright 2020 by Uebert Angel

Published by LEVI HOUSE

Contents

Chapter One
Is there a War against Demons?. 5

Chapter Two
Our Weapons System 20

Chapter Three
The Devil Is Very Small 41

Chapter Four
Jedi Mind Tricks 50

Chapter Five
The Skinny on Spiritual Warfare. 60

Chapter Six
The Influence of the Mind 70

Chapter Seven
When Deliverance Is Needed 78

Chapter Eight
The Intel of Warfare 89

Chapter Nine
Spiritual Thermal Conductivity. 99

Chapter Ten
When Paul Fought the Devil. 111

Contents

Chapter Eleven
Spiritual Kwashiorkor. 117

Chapter Twelve
Resisting the Devil with Spiritual Inertia 126

Chapter Thirteen
Mission Aborted 136

Chapter Fourteen
Unmasking the Devil. 148

Chapter Fifteen
Winning 162

Chapter Sixteen
Unusual Strategies. 172

Chapter One

Is there a War against Demons?

I have heard the voice of Satan, looked dead into his empty face, smelt his breath and heard the callous, prickly, and foul noises of his demonic cohorts. I have seen normal human beings levitate and do things that are not possible physically—speak audibly with their mouths closed, hurl objects around rooms without touching them—all under the influence of this diabolic devil and his cohorts. I have seen the devil himself as clear as I see these pages. The devil is not a hoax. I have seen him, and I know what he is at the core. He is empty!

Once Upon a Time in Rotherham

"Prophet, whatever you do, don't pray for that girl!"

I looked at the pastor perplexed by his request. Apparently, I had started a war that no one was expecting to be waged in that three-day conference. By the time he pulled me closer to himself to try and prevent me from casting out the demons from that lady, she was already walking towards me. This war was being waged in front of the whole congregation. And unbeknownst to me, every minister who had previously attempted to cast the demons out of her were given the "sons of Sceva" treatment. They were embarrassed and 'whooped' in front of the congregation and some beaten to a pulp.

I could see as the lady was approaching the pastor was truly quivering in fear. He feared for my life and my ministry. Then it happened. Unusual for her weight and size, she rolled into a ball in the most peculiar way like a contortionist. That alone sent chills through the crowds, many of whom had seen this before. But as I would learn later, not at the magnitude she now demonstrated.

"I will not get out of her!"

A scratchy but clear voice came out of her without the mouth even moving an inch. I looked at her straight into her eyeballs and adjured the demons to leave.

"You foul spirit, I am here to serve you notice in the name of Jesus, your time in this place is over!"

With those words, animal-like growls, inhuman sounds, guttural, masculine and at most times high pitched came from everywhere around her like a subwoofer with surround system. I knew it was not her mouth but something beyond her. Her eyes expressed hatred for anything me. Such unusual strength came over her that any usher who was trying to help was hurled from her like straw. She wasn't struggling to ward off any restraint they were trying to be. Things in the church building began to move on their own accord. This was by all analysis, something beyond belief. I had touched something, and a very sinister power was afoot in and around that lady.

I looked at her again, this time more at ease than before, and called out "In the name of Jesus, come out of her!" With that, I pointed towards the wall to direct the demonic influence to check out using that as the exit point. For a split second, it seemed the battle had gotten worse. The building wall in the direction I was pointing began to crack and the same wall emitted a cracking sound that sent shock waves among the congregation. She welled up a burst of scornful laughter, and with no words, I pointed at her and then at the wall. That's when the talk of the century in that Rotherham town took place.

The whole building shook, and this loud eerie cracking noise could be heard by all. The crack widened, and pieces of brick and motar fell from within the crack. A big hole appeared in the wall as the demonic forces were vacating. Her balled up body seemed to be floating in the sight of all. A mere tactic by a losing enemy to frighten me into surrendering and leaving him in the house he had been for years. Again I pointed at her then to the wall, and she slumped to the floor as if dead, foaming at the mouth.

The pastor was so astonished that his mouth was ajar for many more minutes after that. I proceeded to talk to her and told her to stand up. It took a few minutes before she was up wondering why she was in front of the congregation. She had no recollection of anything that was happening or had happened from unnatural sounds to levitation to walls cracking.

It was a battle to the onlookers but not to me. This wasn't my first rodeo. As a matter of fact, it's not even the most supernaturally active casting of demons I have ever been involved with. Some experiences, if I would tell of them, would be difficult to believe. They were so insanely supernatural they would cause grown men, ministers of the Gospel, to run for their lives. What shocked me was the number of ministers at that conference who witnessed this deliverance and then came to request the power to be able to do the same. That's when I realised one strange truth which I call the biggest problem of the Church.

The Strange Truth About the Devil and Warfare

The strange truth and biggest problem in the Church today is that many Christians don't know the truth about Satan's defeat. They are unknowingly siding with the devil and aiding him in his deception by believing that he is a powerful foe. The strange truth is the devil is defeated by revelation, not by anything else. You see, you can find a "deliverance" church on every other corner with people queuing up to get involved with some form of "spiritual warfare." People spend hours and days fighting the devil in various ways. But the reality is, Satan has already been defeated. We don't need to defeat him again. Now that can come as a shock to you, but it's a reality many Christians seem to forget.

Now you say, *Wait a minute, Prophet. What about what the Bible calls warfare?*

2 Corinthians 10:4
"The weapons of our warfare..."

I will deal with that as we weave through this straightforward but seemingly difficulty revelation. Now, you need to understand that the word *warfare* has nothing to do with a real war. This word warfare in the Greek is where we get the word *stratos* meaning strategy. So, the war then is a strategic warfare. Stay with me as I shed more light on this.

Before I go deeper on the stratos, let me just pinpoint that a war only exists as long as one of the opponents remains undefeated. As soon as one enemy is conquered, the war is over. Satan is a defeated foe, yet Christians are still at war with him. War, by definition, is a state of conflict between two armed opponents, and the Bible clearly tells us that Satan is unarmed.

Colossians 2:15 says,

"And having spoiled principalities and powers, he made a shew of them openly, triumphing over them in it."

The devil is an entity that the Lord spoiled, and that is *apekdýomai*, that is the Greek word rendered "spoiled" in that verse. It means *to plunder, despoil, disarm*. Jesus didn't only defeat Satan, but He also *spoiled* him. He stripped him of everything he had, completely disarming him of any weapon that he could ever use against us, including hell and death. The scripture tells us that Jesus snatched the keys of hell and death.

Revelation 1:18
I am he that liveth, and was dead; and, behold, I am alive for evermore, Amen; and have the keys of hell and of death.

The devil doesn't even have keys to his final destination, his own house. Hallelujah!

Let's look at Colossians 2:15 again because there is something I need to show you about the word "shew."

9

Colossians 2:15
"And having spoiled principalities and powers, he made a *shew* [emphasis added] of them openly, triumphing over them in it."

Now, the Greek word that was translated "shew" in Colossians 2:15 is *deigmatízō* which means *to exhibit*. *Deigmatízō* comes from the root word *deîgma*, which means *a specimen*. Satan is nothing more than a specimen on exhibit. When I was a young boy in high school, we had a science club, and I loved it so much because it was very practical. We would have dead insects that were impaled, pinned to a board on exhibit for every student to touch and examine at close range. That's the way you need to see the devil: an ugly dead insect pinned to the cross of Jesus; a specimen on display; a bug with no life in it, nowhere to go and no one to harm.

I must add that this is not all Jesus did. There's more to the verse. After He made a shew—a *deigmatízō,* specimen on exhibit—of the devil, the scripture says, **"*triumphing* over them."** The Greek word *thriambeúō* translated "triumphing over" is especially significant. It means *to make an acclamatory procession*. This is specifically referring to the way the Romans had a "triumphant procession" after they had defeated their enemies. This was no small or quiet affair.

Satan Exhibited by Jesus

Now, way back when the Romans would conquer an enemy, they would hold colourful and extravagant parades that would draw everybody's attention. They would completely humiliate the conquered king by stripping him naked and dragging him behind the conquering king or commander for all the crowd to see. And that's not all. They would also cut off both his thumbs and the big toes of both feet so he could never hold a sword again, and he would never be able to run. They would even castrate him so he would not have any children that might grow up and become the conquering king's enemies in the future. The Romans had learnt how to truly humiliate a defeated enemy. They would utterly embarrass him. This was done to show the people there was no need to fear this enemy ever again. He was no longer a threat to anyone.

That's what Jesus did to the devil. Jesus whooped the devil, stripped Him of every weapon, pinned him like a lab specimen, then had a big parade to show everybody that he is a totally conquered foe. But it seems as if many Christians missed the parade. Instead of living in the victory and assurance of the devil's sound defeat, they run around in hushed tones, afraid the devil will hear them, and propagate the lie that Satan is a powerful foe. That's not so!

Yes, Satan is still creeping around, but our dealings with him are primarily because there are so many lies circulating in the Church about his power against us. The only power he has are the lies the Church believes. When we believe his lies, he has the opportunity to use our own authority against us. You see, fear opens the door for him to wreak havoc in our lives. We—the Christians—are the ones with the power. Satan has no power of his own. Instead, he uses the power and authority that our ignorance gives him.

Brothers and sisters, we need to believe that Satan was already completely destroyed. Hebrews 2:14 says:

Forasmuch then as the children are partakers of flesh and blood, he also himself likewise took part of the same; that through death he might destroy him that had the power of death, that is, the devil.

We don't need to fight the devil. All we need to do is to enforce his defeat. Our duty is to stand against the wiles—the trickery—of the devil. The devil is holding an anti-bullying campaign against you. Bullies are notorious for picking fights with the puniest and most defenceless person. When you fight the devil, it's like Rambo strapped with M4 Carbine Commando machine guns blazing, riding full speed in an M1 Abrams battle tank, fully locked and loaded and aimed at a baby in wet diapers with nothing in his hand but a pacifier. A bully fights the one he's sure he can beat, but you are actually worse than a bully because you are fighting someone who was already beaten.

You see, Satan is powerless. All he's got up his sleeve are tricks of deception and bullying. But what makes deception so deceptive is that the deceived person doesn't know they are deceived. If they did, it wouldn't be deception. The only thing that can defeat deception is truth. Once the truth is known and received, deception loses all its power and empties the devil's bag of tricks.

That is what Ephesians 6:11 means when it says:

Put on the whole armour of God, that ye may be able to stand against the wiles of the devil.

Any other approach is actually giving the devil authority and power which he doesn't have. That is what he uses to intimidate. Understand this once and for all: the only weapon Satan has is the power we give him when we believe his lies. We are not at war with the devil, as most preachers are saying. That is the truth that the Body of Christ desperately needs to know in order to be free from the devil's bag of tricks.

Interestingly enough, there is a lot of deliverance taking place in the Church today, a whole lot! One of the trademarks of deliverance churches or centres is that the preacher *delivers* a mic to the devil, allowing him to speak. They *deliver* their attention to demons whose primary goal is to use tricks to distract and disrupt what God is doing. These preachers make themselves willing participants in the devil's trickery, *delivering* themselves over to be hoodwinked by his lies. They *deliver* spiritually immature people over to a level of ignorance surpassed only by their own.

Yes, there's a lot of deliverance taking place! But if they only read their Bible, they would know that the primary character of the devil is that he is a deceiver, a liar, a trickster. Why then would anybody engage in conversation with a personality who is incapable of anything but lies and deception? We were never told to have any conversation with the devil. We were told to cast him out.

Smith Wigglesworth, one of the greatest generals of faith, was delivered from demons by a dog. One day, as he waited at a bus stop, he observed a little dog who had followed its owner. The lady, realising the dog must have followed her from home, was surprised to see the dog at her feet happily wagging its tail. She

13

bent down and patted the dog on its head. "I can't have you with me today. Go home." Sensing only her mild disposition, the dog responded with more enthusiastic tail wagging.

Knowing that the bus would soon arrive, the lady became slightly agitated. "Go home, dear." But the dog, still sensing no real urgency, interpreted her request as a playful gesture and responded in kind. Seeing the bus approaching, the lady abandoned all niceties, stamped her foot, and commanded the dog, "Go home *now*!" The little dog tucked its tail between its legs and took off at once. Smith Wigglesworth caught the revelation and shouted with delight, "That's how you treat the devil!" You see, the dog's response delivered him from his ignorance of how to deal with devils.

Every Sunday, and sometimes twice a week, there is a pastor somewhere negotiating with demonic terrorists. And the terrorists are winning. They are not winning because they are more powerful, no! They are winning because these pastors are allowing the devil to hold hostage the truth that belongs to them, and they are paying him ransom by believing the lie that he is more powerful than they are.

You need to understand that if Jesus had not paralysed Satan, if He hadn't utterly defeated Satan, He would have never been able to come out of the grave. The resurrection is the final proof that Jesus neutralised Satan. He rendered him as useless as a Tesla without batteries. Otherwise, He would have never come out of Hell.

The Bibles lets us know that Jesus went down to Hell and beat the devil on his own territory. The Weymouth translation of Colossians 2:15 says:

Colossians 2:15
And the hostile princes and rulers He shook off from Himself.

Hallelujah! The devil and his cohorts grabbed hold of Jesus, and He just shook them off like bothersome gnats!

Jesus went into Hell and came out of Hell. Do you understand how powerful that is? He went into Hell *and* had the nerve, the audacity, the spiritual temerity to come back out. Boy, I love this Jesus! Not only that, but then He handed the victory over to us, the same victory with which he overcame Satan. His victory is our victory! That's why in Mark 16:17, He says:

Mark 16:17
In my name shall they cast out devils.

He said in My name you shall *cast out* devils! Glory to God! Let me explain why you need to get excited about that.

The word there for 'cast out' is the Greek word *ekbállō* which means to *expel, cast out, drive out*. But most Christians don't understand what this means. They think it means to wrestle. That is one of the reasons you have people spending hours doing "deliverance," wrestling with demons, going back and forth exchanging pleasantries.

"Come out!"
"I'm not coming out!"
"In the name of Jesus, you are coming out today, by fire, by thunder, in the name of Jesus!"

And three hours later, they are still handing the devil the mic. This is an error! We do not negotiate with terrorists.

I know some of you are saying, *Well, the Bible says we should wrestle*. Let me tell you something, we are not commanded to wrestle with the devil. We are commanded to stand against his tricks. Ephesians 6:11 says it this way:

Ephesians 6:11
Put on the whole armour of God, that ye may be able to stand against the wiles of the devil.

We don't wrestle with the devil; we stand. Standing is the only wrestling we are required to do. We don't tolerate, interrogate, or placate devils; we kick them out.

Let me show you what it's like to ekbállō devils. Imagine yourself walking down Bond Street in London, your brand new Vincenzo Luca limited-edition handcrafted Italian leather shoes gleaming in the sunlight. Suddenly, a gust of wind blows a torn page from the Financial Review. Soiled with muck and filth, it lands on your right shoe. With a swift knee-jerk response, you react to the nuisance and kick the rubbish aside. *That's* how you cast out devils. It's not a battle. It's simply a spiritual knee-jerk response to a piece of rubbish devil that happens to be in your way.

Ekbállō is not conditional, neither is it optional. It forces compliance. Ekbállō violates the laws of physics. Newton's third law states that for every action, there is an equal and opposite reaction. This law maintains that whatever force you use, an equal and opposite force pushes back at you. But when it comes to ekbállō—kicking out devils—this law can't work because it is an out-of-balance situation. There is no equal and opposite force in that scenario because when you cast out devils, there is only one force with power involved and that's Jesus.

In Mark chapter 9, we have the account of the father who brought his son to Jesus. The son was possessed with a dumb spirit, and that thing was wreaking havoc in his life. Many times that devil would throw him in the fire or drown him. But I want you to see how powerless the devil and his cohorts are.

The scripture says that Jesus commanded the boy to be brought to Him. Now, some might think, Oh, this is a powerful demon. It robbed this child of his hearing and his ability to speak. And it would force him into fire and water. But watch what it says in the first part of verse 20:

Mark 9:20
And they brought him unto Him...

If this devil was as powerful as it seemed, why did it allow itself to be brought to Jesus? If it were powerful, shouldn't it be able to resist? The scripture says, "*they*" brought him unto Him. That tells you right there that this devil couldn't even resist the ones who brought him to Jesus. As long as Jesus is involved, devils don't have the option to resist.

Now, I want you to see what happens next. Let's finish verse 20:

Mark 9:20
And they brought him unto Him: and when he saw Him, straightway the spirit tare him; and he fell on the ground, and wallowed foaming.

That's what it looks like when a devil encounters the power of Jesus: it threw a tantrum! That devil threw that boy into convulsions, and he was rolling around on the ground foaming at the mouth like a rabid mad dog. If something like that happened in the presence of some preachers who don't understand how powerless the devil is, they might suddenly have the urge to turn the service over to someone else and make a hasty exit. But not Jesus. He didn't even flinch. He stood flat-footed and calm. He wasn't moved in the least by those devilish dramatics. You see, He knew that devils like attention. So, His response was to ignore the empty noise and calmly continue His conversation with the boy's father. Watch what it says in verse 21:

Mark 9:21
And He asked his father, How long is it ago since this came unto him? And he said, Of a child.

It was only when the crowd began to gather to see what the commotion was all about that Jesus diffused the situation and commanded the dumb and deaf spirit to come out.

Mark 9:25
When Jesus saw that the people came running together, he rebuked the foul spirit, saying unto him, Thou dumb and deaf spirit, I charge thee, come out of him, and enter no more into him.

Now, I want you to notice what happened when Jesus commenced to ekbállō this deaf and dumb spirit. Things appeared to get worse. Watch what verse 26 says:

Mark 9:26
And the spirit cried, and rent him sore, and came out of him:
and he was as one dead; insomuch that many said, He is dead.

When Jesus commanded that devil out, it began to let out a loud, high-pitched scream and threw the boy into convulsions. But no matter how much noise that thing made or how violent the reaction, the next five words tell us how to *logízomai*—conclude—the whole matter: "**and came out of him**." Devils may make noise when you ekbállō them, but they'll make it on their way *out*!

Ekbállō takes no prisoners. When you use the name of Jesus and kick a devil out, it has no choice but to go. It has met an irresistible force! The old preacher of renown, Dr S.M. Lockridge, declared of Jesus, *He's indescribable! He's incomprehensible. He's invincible. He's irresistible*! That devil may even try to hide. But when ekbállō is involved, brother, it's like what the children say in the game of hide and seek: *ready or not, here I come*! That devil has to go!

When you kick an object out of the way, that object cannot turn around and tell you, "I'm not going." There is irresistible force involved. It has no more power to resist than that rubbish piece of paper that was kicked out of the way. It has no choice but to go. Jesus didn't say in My name you shall *negotiate* with devils. He said cast out, kick out—*ekbállō* devils!

Chapter Two

Our Weapons System

The Lockheed Martin F-35 Lightning II is a 5th generation single-seat fighter jet. It combines some of the most advanced weaponry and stealth capability in the world. Its unparalleled stealth technology allows it to go undetected by even the most sophisticated radars. And if you can't see it, you can't stop it. Advanced electronic warfare enables the F-35 to locate and track enemy forces, jam radars and disrupt attacks with unparalleled effectiveness. It can carry up to six air-to-surface missiles, and it dominates the air with a top speed of 1.6 Mach, that's 1.6 times the speed of sound.

Without question, the F-35 is designed for total mission success and the most survivable yet lethal cockpit environment to date. With the most expensive weapons system in military history, the F-35 is the most advanced fighter jet in the world, a gamechanger, a beast in the air. But with all its sophisticated weaponry, it can't do a thing underwater. Its weapons system is not designed for underwater warfare; it's designed for aerial warfare.

You see, your weapons determine your warfare. In other words, the only way to know the kind of spiritual warfare in which you're engaged is to understand the type of weapons you're given. Ephesians chapter 6 describes for us the weapons system of the Christian, but we have a juvenile revelation of it. That's why so many Christians are crying for deliverance and fighting with the devil. Only foolish people fight the devil. Foolishness means you lack pertinent information. And if you are fighting the devil, you will definitely need deliverance, not from the devil but from your own ignorance.

If you know Jesus defeated the devil and you're still fighting him, you are deluded; you lack reality. But today is your day. You are about to be part of the most powerful deliverance session you could ever imagine, and you won't even have to roll on the floor or vomit. You will be made free by the knowledge of the truth.

Now, let's take a look at this weapons system so we can be clear about the type of warfare in which we are engaged. The scripture starts off this way in Ephesians 6, verse 10:

Ephesians 6:10
Finally, my brethren, be strong in the Lord, and in the power of his might.

Do you see the word 'fight' in that verse? It's not there, because the warfare in which the Christian is engaged has nothing to do with fighting whatsoever. It says, be strong—*endynamóō* (empowered)—in or by the Lord, and in the *krátos* of His *ischýs*. That speaks of power you get from the Word. I have dealt with this at length in my book *Supernatural Power of the Believer: The Secrets to Growing in the Five Dimensions of God's Power.* Read it!

The thing I want you to notice in that verse is that neither the strength, the power or the might is generated by you. That tells you right from the start that the success of this type of warfare which I'm about to explain is not about how powerful or strong you are or how well you can fight the devil. I repeat. This warfare does not require you to fight, not one bit. So, let's read on to see how we are equipped for this warfare.

Verse 11 goes on to tell us about the components of our weapons system. The Bible calls it "the whole armour of God." Let's read it.

Ephesians 6:11
Put on the whole armour of God, that ye may be able to stand against the wiles of the devil.

It says, "put on," *endýō* (in the Greek), which means *sink down into it*; drown in the armour of God. When you sink into something, it means you go beneath the surface of that thing. The Church in large part has had only a surface understanding of the armour of God, a juvenile revelation of it. Until you put on—*endýō*—the *whole* armour of God, you cannot do what the next part of the verse is saying.

Let me explain it this way. A shoe is not only made for walking, but it is also designed to protect the foot. If you give a two-year-old a shoe, he may put it in his mouth, on top of his head, or put his hand in there. Why? Because he does not fully understand what a shoe is and what it is for. If he steps on a stone, he could bring harm to himself because the shoe is not on his foot. So he becomes vulnerable to something that was never supposed to affect him.

It's not because the thing he stepped on is more powerful than he is, but because he did not make proper use of that which he was given to make him invulnerable. Similarly, when you don't understand what the armour of God is and what it's for, you will misuse it or not use it at all. That misuse or non-use causes you to become vulnerable to that which should never affect you at all.

So the verse says, sink down into the armour. In other words, go beyond a surface understanding of what the armour is and what it's for, *so that* you may be able to stand. Notice, you can't do the standing part until you've done the sinking down into it part. One is the prerequisite of the other. That's why the verse says that you *may* be able to stand. It doesn't say you *will* be able to stand; it's not a clear-cut thing. You cannot stand until you put on—*endýō*, sink down into, go beyond the surface understanding of—the armour of God.

Now, here follows a crucial part of the verse where it says:

...That ye may be able to *stand against the wiles of the devil* [emphasis added].

The first thing I want you to note is that you are not fighting against the wiles of the devil. You are standing from a position of victory which you have already attained. That means the purpose of the warfare is not to win. You have already won in Christ. The purpose is to stand, maintain your position of victory. I will say more about that, but first let's finish this verse.

The Methodia of the Devil

Note this, Paul is telling us we have to stand against the *wiles* of the devil. Now, the word *wiles* there does not mean weapons. It is the word *methodeía* from which we get the word Methodist or method. In the Greek rendering, it means *tricks*. That means that the enemy you are fighting only has tricks, no power. Magicians call it sleight of hand. If you read my wife's book, *Grace Driven Life*, she talks about the sleight of hand magicians who use speed to deceive.

Scientifically, it's impossible for any human being to multitask. Your mind cheats you into thinking you're multitasking, but in reality, it's just moving very fast from one thing to the other. So because there is so much speed, you think you are multitasking, but you're really multi-switching. Nobody on earth can multitask according to science.

Men know exactly what I'm talking about. They can't multitask. A woman can rock the baby to sleep, fry the sausage, and answer the phone, deftly switching from one task to the other. A man will fry the baby, answer the sausage, and rock the phone to sleep. We can't do it. Nobody can multitask unless it's by the Holy Ghost. The natural mind cannot.

So magicians use sleight of hand by taking advantage of the fact that the mind cannot multitask. They lead you to *believe* you are concentrating on the trick they are performing, knowing that you are really focusing on something else. While your attention is still on the trick you *think* is happening, they are quickly doing something else. By the time your mind switches to what they were doing, the trick has already been done. When this happens, people are shocked because their eyes were wide open, and they thought they saw everything. They never saw everything. They missed the trick because their minds could not focus on two things at the same time.

So, the devil does not have power. He's using tricks! He came to Eve and said, *Eve, did God say?* What was he trying to do? He was trying to get information about what God said. He didn't know. You think he was referring to the tree in the middle of the Garden of Eden, but he didn't know which tree it was. Look at what he said:

Genesis 3:1
Now the serpent was more subtil than any beast of the field which the Lord God had made. And he said unto the woman, Yea, hath God said, Ye shall not eat of *every* tree of the garden [emphasis added]?

Notice, he said of *every* tree. That tells you he didn't even know which tree. It was Eve who said not *every* tree, but *that* particular tree, the one in the midst of the garden.

Genesis 3:2-3
And the woman said unto the serpent, We may eat of the fruit of the trees of the garden: But of the fruit of the tree which is in the midst of the garden, God hath said, Ye shall not eat of it, neither shall ye touch it, lest ye die.

Eve was tricked into surrendering that information, and she didn't even realise she was being tricked. After she released that information, she ate of the fruit then took it to Adam, and he ate, and immediately they lost the power. The whole thing went bad based on what she told the devil.

25

That is the kind of trickery he uses. It's all about deception, and it only works if you are oblivious to spiritual warfare. The only way the devil can take power from you is by tricking you into thinking you have no power and that he has more power than you. He knows, in actual fact, that you are the one with the power, and he has no power.

Now someone will say what about the part in Luke 10:19 where the Lord Jesus says, **I give you power over all the power of the devil**. Some will say, *Prophet, right there it says we have power over all the power of the devil*. But I want you to see something here. The first "power" is not the same as the second "power." They are two different words in the Greek: *exousía* (authority) and *dunamis* (inherent power or ability to cause changes). So, God is saying I give you authority to stop the power of the devil. In other words, exousía has more power because it stops the power you surrendered to the devil from working. You see, the devil lied, and he got our power. So if you understood what the Lord is telling us, it would read like this in your spirit:

I give you authority to nullify all the power the devil took from you through his lies and deception.

You see, when Eve fell prey to the devil's trickery and convinced Adam to eat of the fruit, the devil was given power of attorney to act in Adam's place. This is the reason why the devil could appear in Heaven before a God who has no appreciation of evil, and nothing happened to him. He was using Adamic authority. He was using the power of attorney of Adam just as we use the power of attorney of Jesus here on earth and in the spiritual realm. But when Jesus came, that power of attorney ended.

The only problem is that some Christians never read the memo. They still think the devil has power, so they need some kind of deliverance so they can roll on the floor.

Wrestling with Spiritual Powers

Listen, Jesus can be present, and you still live a life of deficiency, wrestling life's vicissitudes. It's not that He hasn't already given you everything you need to live a victorious life, but it's because you are ignorant. And you remain that way because you'd rather oppose God and think He hasn't given you everything than to admit your ignorance.

Let's go to verse 12:

Ephesians 6:12
For we wrestle not against flesh and blood, but against principalities, against powers, against the rulers of the darkness of this world, against spiritual wickedness in high places.

The Bible says we "wrestle not." I know you're saying, *Wait a minute, Prophet. You just told us we're not fighting. Now you're telling us we are wrestling.* You're missing the point. You're still looking at it from the perspective of the natural. The verse is telling us that we are *not* wrestling against flesh and blood. So if it's not flesh and blood, even when you're praying physically, why are you sending fire to the person you see as your enemy? Imagine how many times you've done it, and your enemy is still succeeding. You sent lightning, fire, even thunder, and two weeks later, your enemy is buying a Mercedes.

Your problem is not your brother or sister. You're not wrestling against human beings but against "principalities, against powers, against the rulers of the darkness of this world, against spiritual wickedness in high places." These are demonic forces. But what you need to notice here is that it says we *wrestle* not. There's something about the wrestling we need to realise. This is not a fight, as some would suppose. Remember, you're already the champion. All the enemy is trying to do is trick you into thinking you're not. The Bible says in Romans 8:37:

Romans 8:37
Yet in all these things we are more than conquerors

In other words, a conqueror is the one who goes out and wins. But the one who is "more than a conqueror" has done all his fighting and is sitting at a beach somewhere sipping on juice, enjoying the sunshine, and enjoying his victory loot. He has finished doing victory laps. He leaves that for the conquerors for he or she is a more than a conqueror.

Understanding Spiritual Wrestling

In the sport of wrestling, there is a tactic called pinning your opponent where you hold down or pin your opponent's shoulders onto the mat. You neutralise him by immobilising him to stop him from further attacking you. This is where some Christians get it wrong. They fight the devil thinking they are preventing him from attacking. But remember, the devil was already pinned. The Bible tells us in Colossians 2:15 that Jesus spoiled principalities and powers and pinned the devil like a lab specimen and put him on display for everyone to see.

Colossians 2:15
And having spoiled (*disarmed*) principalities and powers, he made a shew of them openly, triumphing over them in it.

Brothers and sisters, you don't have to pin the devil. Jesus already did that. All you're doing is keeping him in that pinned position. We do not wrestle to obtain the victory. We wrestle to maintain the victory that Jesus already obtained for us. Hallelujah!

One day in the Harare International Conference Centre, a demon-possessed lady walked straight to me, grabbed the mic, threw it across the room and began to speak gibberish and cussing me out in all vulgarity. I looked at her until I realised I was giving her attention and the devil likes attention, so I proceeded to where the mic had been thrown. But before I picked up the mic, I heard God speak to me as clear as day, and He said:

"Why are you letting a defeated enemy send you across the room?"

I turned on the spot in front of over five thousand people, on live tv and commanded the demoniac to go pick up the mic herself. She obeyed the name of Jesus with speed and brought back my mic. When she brought it, it wasn't as clean as before, so I commanded her to clean it. The devil begged for mercy right there, cleaning the mic until it was sparkling clean. But with usual ease, I told him to leave because I caught the revelation. I wrestle differently. I wrestle the Word way.

Now You might be wondering, *Well, what kind of wrestling are we doing*? I'm glad you asked. Let's go back to Ephesians 6 and look at verse 13 to find out. It says:

Ephesians 6:13
Wherefore take unto you the whole armour of God, that ye may be able to withstand in the evil day, and having done all, to stand.

The first thing I want you to notice is that it says we should take the *whole* armour, not a little bit, not part of it but the whole thing. Does it say that when you take the whole armour you should fight and wrestle or do anything physical? No, it does not! But just imagine the number of Christians who are wasting their physical energy in spiritual warfare.

Are you telling me you're more powerful than what Jesus did to defeat the enemy? When you fight the devil, you're implying that there are some things Jesus left undone that you need to correct. So, is deliverance necessary? Yes! Is it for mature Christians? Never! The Bible tells us that the devil is under our feet. For you to fight him, you have to take him from under your feet, make him stand up, and tell him his defeat by Jesus is not enough, so let's fight again. Do you see how absurd that is? The greatest deliverance is when your ignorance is confronted!

Verse 13 also talks about something called "the evil day." There is a revelation there that many people have not understood. Let's look at the verse again.

Ephesians 6:13
Wherefore take unto you the whole armour of God, that ye may be able to withstand in the evil day...

The evil day is not optional. It's coming. One of the greatest outcries is why do bad things happen to good people. People wonder *if this one is a man of God or woman of God, why is evil coming?* The Bible says without equivocation, there is an evil day. That is a prophecy that will never fail. The evil day is coming. So Paul tells us we need the whole armour so that we can withstand the evil day. What proves you're a man or woman of God is not that the evil day doesn't come. It's that the evil day comes and you're still smiling in the eye of the storm.

In Heaven, I don't want to be the only general with no wounds to talk about. When generals are telling their stories, comparing former scars and how they were persecuted for God's work, I don't want to be the only general with no story to tell. Notice, if demons are still your trouble, you are still small. When you are big, governments sit down and hold meetings because of you.

I remember arriving at a certain airport, and the wife of the president of that country was waiting there to keep me from entering the country. They even called the president, and he told them if it's Angel, never let him into this country. I was so honoured. I said boys, we have graduated! I later got wind that they had sat in parliament to talk about me and to discuss my arrival, and the ruling party had its way. When it's only Shénaynay and Ray-Ray talking about you, you are still little. Let the *Telegraph* begin to talk about you; let *The New York Times* begin to persecute you. That's when you know you've graduated.

So, the evil day is coming, but it should find you suited and booted in the whole amour. And what are you doing? You are withstanding, and the word withstand does not mean to fight back. It means to be invincible. You are standing, and there's a wall that protects you so the enemy can't come close. Ephesians 6, verse 13 going into verse 14 says:

Ephesians 6:13b – 14a
And having done all, to stand. Stand therefore...

Having done all to stand, what do we do, fight? Wrestle? No! After you've stood, the next step is to keep standing.

Remember, I started this chapter by telling you that the type of weapons described in Ephesians chapter 6 will determine whether spiritual warfare is real. Let me illustrate.

> One man says to the other, "An enemy is coming, and he's very dangerous."
> "Whoa! Is he dangerous? Okay. How should I defend myself?"
> "Just use a mango. You don't even need to use the whole mango. A piece of it is enough."
> "Do I need to throw the mango?"
> "No, just hold it."

How dangerous can this enemy be if all you need to do to ward him off is hold a mango! You would know based on the choice of weapon that this enemy can't be nearly as dangerous as he was believed to be.

Now, in the light of that illustration, let's continue reading about the weapons described for us starting in Ephesians 6, verse 14:

Ephesians 6:14
Stand therefore, *having your loins girt about with truth* **[emphasis added], and having on the breastplate of righteousness;**

So, truth is a weapon, but what kind of weapon is it? What can you do with it? You just need to know the truth. Jesus said, "**I am the truth**" (John 14:6). Then Paul goes on to say, "**having on the breastplate of righteousness**." How do we get righteousness? The Bible says it's a gift. There is nothing you need to do. Your righteousness is not based on your good works, how good you've been, or whether you've done everything right. Your righteousness is not *like* Christ's, it *is* Christ's. You have *His* righteousness.

Let me just point out right here that nobody on earth is more righteous than another. Some preachers will lie to you to get you to come to church under the guise that by doing so, you will become more righteous. There is no such thing as getting more righteousness. You can increase in *fruits* of righteousness, but you can never increase in righteousness.

I was born in Africa. When I became a British citizen, I received a red passport. One of my pastors, who happens to be white, was born in Middlesbrough in North-eastern England. He also has a red passport. Though he is a born native of England, his passport is no redder than mine. We have the same benefits. Now, imagine righteousness as a passport you've been given. It doesn't need to become redder than anyone else's any more than you need to become more righteous. Understanding that you're already righteous is what will keep the devil from playing tricks on you.

Now, let's look at another component of our weapons system. Verse 15 says:

Ephesians 6:15
And your feet shod with the preparation of the gospel of peace;

The Gospel of Peace is winning souls. That's part of the whole armour. So if you spend one year without winning souls, there is an open door for the enemy to enter, a chink in your armour. Winning souls is something you must be actively doing.

Proverbs 11:30 says "**he that winneth souls is wise.**" That's not up for debate; that's just the truth. The converse is also true: he that does not win souls is foolish, a nincompoop, a dunderhead. This is no juvenile revelation. This is for those who are mature. We are dealing here with something profound.

Verse 29 of Proverbs 11 tells us:

Proverbs 11:29
He that troubleth his own house shall inherit the wind: and the fool shall be servant to the wise of heart.

Then it immediately follows with "he that winneth souls is wise." What is that telling you? It's telling you that if you are a fool you will become broke, a slave to the wise, the one who wins souls.

Jesus told His disciples to go out and win souls, but they were told not to take anything with them—no wallets, no money, no provisions. When they came back, Jesus asked, "**Did you lack anything?**" They responded, "**Nothing.**" (Luke 22:35). When God gives you a vision to go and win souls, the Bible is saying God will provide.

You wonder, *Why am I broke?* There's a chink in the armour because you're not winning souls. Provision comes from what you're doing in the Kingdom. The moment you start working in God's company, money is coming.

How can you call yourself a Christian and you haven't won one person to Christ? Winning souls brings prosperity, gives somebody who was in darkness light, and closes the chink in your armour. Go out there and win souls! That's a part of your armour, but it's not yet the whole thing. Let's examine the remaining parts.

Paul continues with the armour in verse 16, which says:

Ephesians 6:16
Above all, taking the shield of faith, wherewith ye shall be able to quench all the fiery darts of the wicked.

This verse lets us know that there is something that is "above all," the shield of faith. The Bible tells us that faith comes by hearing and hearing by the Word of God (Romans 10:17). And the Word of God is Truth which, if you are a Christian, you already have. The moment you receive Jesus, you get truth and righteousness. Now we're being told that faith is only to *quench* not to get anything.

35

The reality is, we already have all things. 2 Peter 1:3 tells us that His divine power has already given us all things that pertain to righteousness and unto life. They are all given to you, "for all things are yours" (1 Corinthians 3:21). Are you seeing this? Ephesians 6:15 says with the shield of faith, we are able to *quench* the fiery darts. Notice that we are not using faith to launch weapons. We are not throwing anything. Do you understand? The wicked are the ones firing; we're not firing at anyone. So, how do we use the shield of faith in warfare? By knowing that all things are already yours.

The only way that can happen is by hearing the Word of God. You must keep hearing the Word because your faith can only be fed from hearing the Word. Expose yourself to the Word by searching the scriptures. Go to church, which the Bible calls the pillar and ground of the truth.

1 Timothy 3:15
But if I tarry long, that thou mayest know how thou oughtest to behave thyself in *the house of God, which is the church of the living God, the pillar and ground of the truth* [emphasis added].

1 Corinthians 12:28 tells us that God has chosen ministers who He has brought into the house of God to bless us with the Word and teach us so faith can come to us. These are sources of the Word of God that you need to take advantage of.

Let's move on to verse 17.

Ephesians 6:17
And take the helmet of salvation...

Salvation is *sozo*, which means *nothing missing, nothing broken*. And the location of where you wear a helmet tells you what it protects: your mind.

You need to understand that salvation is not one thing. It has wells in it. The book of Isaiah says it this way:

Isaiah 12:3
Therefore with joy shall ye draw water out of the wells of salvation.

Which well of salvation are you drinking from? You think salvation is just being born again. You believe that one. Yet the same verse that talks about salvation also talks about healing. But some Christians take salvation (i.e. being born again) and leave healing. Your conscience has to be filled with the understanding that you are already covered. You are spiritually, mentally, physically, and financially well. There is nothing missing, and nothing broken.

Now, when it comes to the whole armour, the average Christian will stop at verse 17 of Ephesians 6. But it doesn't stop there. Verse 18 continues:

Ephesians 6:18
Praying always with all prayer and supplication in the Spirit, and watching thereunto with all perseverance and supplication for all saints

Praying in the Spirit and praying for all saints are part of the armour. Now, when people hear "praying in the spirit," they think it means praying in tongues, but that's not true. The Bible talks about walking in the Spirit. Does that mean walking in tongues? We understand from looking at other verses that walking in the Spirit means walking in love. I speak about this at length in my book *Hello Holy Spirit.* So, if walking in the Spirit is walking in love, then praying in the Spirit is praying in love. That rules out the "back to sender" kind of prayer that some Christians use when they claim they are praying "warfare prayers." Back to sender prayers are not part of the armour. Praying in love and interceding for all saints is.

So, if you want your armour to be tight, you have truth (Jesus), righteousness (His gift to you), preach the Gospel (that's winning souls), faith (hearing the Word), salvation (knowing what salvation has given you), praying in love and for all saints (intercession). If you have these things, the devil can't defeat you. But there is one more piece of the armour I need to tell you about.

Ephesians 6:19 says this:

Ephesians 6:19
And for me, that utterance may be given unto me, that I may open my mouth boldly, to make known the mystery of the gospel,

Praying for your man of God or woman of God is also part of the armour. Without it, your armour is incomplete. And I want you to notice what Paul says we should pray for. Let's look at verses 19 through 21:

Ephesians 6:19-21
And for me, that utterance may be given unto me, that I may open my mouth boldly, to make known the mystery of the

gospel, For which I am an ambassador in bonds: that therein I may speak boldly, as I ought to speak. But that ye also may know my affairs, and how I do, Tychicus, a beloved brother and faithful minister in the Lord, shall make known to you all things:

Paul is not saying to pray for boldness. When you receive the Holy Ghost you already have boldness, so you don't need to pray for that. Only a fool begs for what he already owns. But he says to pray **"that ye may also *know* my affairs and how I do."** He says, know (*eido*), be aware of my needs. That's the kind of prayer he's talking about. *Eido* my needs, meaning have a spiritual awareness of what the man and woman of God need. Pray for your man or woman of God and for the servants of God around the world. That's part of your armour.

Paul was not afraid to make his financial needs known. And just in case the people were not spiritually aware of what he needed, there was a guy named Tychicus who knew what Paul needed and communicated that to the churches all over. That means giving to the needs of your man and woman of God is also part of the armour.

Now you've seen what is in your weapons system, the whole armour. As long as the components of the armour are in place, they form an impenetrable wall around you. Of course, the devil still skulks around looking for any chinks in the armour. He tries to attack using tricks, but they can only work if you negotiate on one of these components of the armour.

Let me give you an example. Let's say the devil goes to the part of the armour that has to do with giving to your man or woman of God. He may come to you as a Christian and tell you, *Oh, these people are just stealing your money. That's all they want.* Then you, believing the lie of the devil, decide not to give anymore. When you do that, you compromise the weapon of giving to the needs of your man or woman of God. That creates a chink in the armour, an open door for the devil to come in. That's when the fighting begins: you fight him, and he fights you. Why? Because a part of your armour is missing.

So, is deliverance necessary? Yes, but only when the devil lies to you, and you agree with him. By doing so, you create a chink in your armour and compromise the integrity of your weapons system.

Chapter Three

The Devil Is Very Small

Spiritual warfare, the way most Christians understand it, is the snake oil that the devil is selling, and preachers have become his salesforce. These preachers believe that spiritual warfare is the remedy to what ails them. They think that without it, they will succumb to the power of the devil.

There are only two lies the devil wants you to believe. One is that he doesn't exist. The other is that he is so powerful, and I mean more than you. Most Christians vehemently reject the first lie—they believe the devil exists. But they have swallowed the lie that the devil is powerful hook, line, sinker, the boat, the fisherman, his boots and the green he is sitting on! This is why so many Christians are wasting their time, energy, and prayers on what they believe to be spiritual warfare.

Most Christian preachers worship the devil every Sunday. They mount the pulpit, pick up the Holy Bible, and then proceed to declare what can only be described as the "wondrous works" of the devil. They talk about how terrible and wicked the devil is, and how much of a liar he is. They laud his character, speaking at length about who he is and what he does, which is precisely what we understand worship to be.

When you listen to some preachers, you would be confused about whether they are talking about the devil or Jesus. They spend more time talking about what the devil is doing than what God is doing. And when they talk about what they believe the devil can do, they speak in hushed, reverent tones as though they are afraid the devil might hear them. The funny thing is, while they are busy saying the devil did this or that, he is standing on the sidelines crying "It wasn't me!"

The devil is everything God is not, though he is *not* the opposite of God. God has no opposite because He has no equal. He is incomparable. The devil is merely the embodiment of the absence of all that God is. God is Light, illumination, Wisdom. The devil, on the other hand, is referred to as the Prince of Darkness. Prince means *first of*, and darkness does not mean the absence of light. It refers to the lack of illumination, which is *ignorance.* So the devil is the first to be ignorant.

God has perfect knowledge of all things, past, present, and future. The devil only knows what he is told either by action or observation. When God speaks, He articulates wisdom, and that wisdom can only be understood through the agency of the Holy Spirit. The Bible says the natural man cannot understand the things of the Spirit. It's not possible. Watch what the Bible says in 1 Corinthians 2:14:

1 Corinthians 2:14 AMPC
But the natural, nonspiritual man does not accept or welcome or admit into his heart the gifts and teachings and revelations of the Spirit of God, for they are folly (meaningless nonsense) to him; and he is incapable of knowing them [of progressively

recognising, understanding, and becoming better acquainted with them] because they are spiritually discerned and estimated and appreciated.

It takes a regenerated spirit to understand the things of God. The natural man has the possibility of becoming born of the Spirit. But until that happens, he cannot understand the things of God. The devil, on the other hand, has no chance whatsoever of ever becoming a regenerated spirit. He can never understand the things of God. It's not possible! As a created being, he is left with a measure of intelligence, but he's no better than a dog who learns commands by repetition or a lab rat that over time learns how to make its way out of a maze.

The devil is not as smart as you think he is. God can never be duped. You can't outsmart Him no way, no how. But the devil, though he is a deceiver, can be deceived. When you rejoice when things aren't going the way you want them to, you fool the devil into thinking everything is okay with you. When you testify before you see the physical evidence or manifestation of a thing, as far as the devil knows, it's as good as done. That's why the Bible tells us that we overcome by the word of our testimony.

Revelation 12:11
And they overcame him by the blood of the Lamb, and by the word of their testimony

We overcome, *nikáō* in the Greek, which means we *conquer, overcome, prevail, get the victory* when we testify. That's where a lot of Christians miss it. They wait until they see the full manifestation of a thing, *then* they testify. But the scripture tells us that the way we prevail and get the victory over the devil is by testifying. If you look back at verse 10, you will see that the "him" that is spoken of in verse 11 is Satan, the "accuser of the brethren."

Revelation 12:10-11
And I heard a loud voice saying in heaven, Now is come salvation, and strength, and the kingdom of our God, and the power of his Christ: *for the accuser of our brethren* **is cast down, which accused them before our God day and night. And they overcame** *him* **by... the word of their testimony [emphasis added]**

The devil has no idea of the things God has planned for you. He can surmise that something good is getting ready to happen when he sees angelic activity around you. But without a clue, the devil is clueless! And sometimes even with clues, he still can't figure things out. With all the prophetic clues that were given concerning Jesus' death on the cross, the devil still couldn't figure out what was happening because the wisdom of God is beyond the scope of his limited intelligence. Paul says it this way in 1 Corinthians 2:7-8:

1 Corinthians 2:7-8
But we speak the wisdom of God in a mystery, even the hidden wisdom, which God ordained before the world unto our glory: Which none of the princes of this world knew: for *had they known it, they would not have crucified the Lord of glory* **[emphasis added].**

You see, the devil is powerless. Christ resurrecting from the dead is proof that the devil did not have the power to keep Him in Hell. As a matter of fact, the devil couldn't even kill Jesus. The Bible clearly tells us that the devil had nothing to do with Jesus dying. Jesus Himself said, no man can take my life from Me. We find that in John 10:17 and 18:

John 10:17-18
Therefore doth My Father love Me, because *I lay down my life*, that I might take it again. *No man taketh it from me*, but I lay it down of myself. I have power to lay it down, and I have power to take it again. This commandment have I received of my Father [emphasis added].

The devil couldn't kill Jesus. No, not at all! He doesn't have the power to kill anybody. And I know you're thinking, but the verse says "no *man* takes it from me," and the devil is not a man. That's where you would be wrong. That's not what the verse says. The word for 'man' there is *oudeís*, and it means *nobody* or *nothing at all.* That includes the devil. He couldn't kill Jesus, and he can't kill you either.

God is Love personified; the devil is hatred personified. God loves you with perfect love, and the devil hates you with perfect hatred. But you sitting right there reading this book is proof that even though the devil hates you with perfect hatred, he doesn't have the power to kill you. If he could have done it, he would have. The fact is, he can't. He doesn't have the power to do it unless you, by the words of your mouth or otherwise foolish actions, give him the opportunity to work against you.

There is another point I want you to consider so that you can realise once and for all that the devil is nothing to be afraid of. The only person in this universe and beyond who is all-powerful is God. Not only is He all-powerful, but He is also immune to fear. Fear is allergic to God; it can't get anywhere near Him. His God-ness rejects and repels fear. Fear cannot coexist with Love, who God is, any more than light can coexist with darkness. In the book of 1 John, the apostle says it like this:

1 John 4:18, 8
There is no fear in love; but perfect love casteth out fear: because fear hath torment. He that feareth is not made perfect in love. For God is love.

The devil, being the embodiment of what God is not, is powerless and full of fear. That means, according to the verses we just read, the devil is full of torment. Most Christians are afraid of the devil, but the reality is, the devil is terrified of you and with good cause.

You are a God carrier, the ambassador of God on earth. You carry His DNA, His image and His likeness. You look like Him, and you function like Him. Even if you don't realise this, the devil does, and he's terrified! The only problem is preachers who have amplified and magnified the devil and made him seem like this huge force. But the Bible says, when we shall be given the chance to see him, we shall *narrowly* look upon him. That's Isaiah 14:16:

Isaiah 14:16
They that see thee shall narrowly look upon thee, and consider thee, saying, Is this the man that made the earth to tremble, that did shake kingdoms;

When most Christians read that verse, they read it as though they will be the ones shaking at the sight of the devil. That's not the case. Don't for one moment think that when that time comes, we will be looking at the devil in horror. No! The word "see" there is the Hebrew word *raáh*, which means to *enjoy, joyfully, gaze*. We're going to enjoy looking at this tiny thing that so many Christians have been afraid of.

The Bible says we'll have to *narrowly look* (*shagach* in the Hebrew). That means we'll have to squint our eyes to see him because he's so small. If you look at someone narrowly, you look at them in a concentrated way, often because you think they are not giving you full information about something. On that day, you'll look at the devil and think, *is this all there is*?

Spending Hours in Spiritual Warfare

Spending hours in spiritual warfare is the order of the day because people have no idea what warfare means. Warfare, as aforementioned, is where we get the word stratos meaning strategy. If your warfare is not a strategy warfare, then you are not in spiritual warfare. You are too deep in error, wasting your time.

Let me tell a story that happened in the summer of 2010 in Southern Africa. I was called to attend to a demoniac with peculiar abilities that had amazed and frightened the spectators, which included pastors and bishops. Two bishops and three pastors were there with the mother of the young boy, and everyone was in shock. No one wanted to be next to the boy.

As soon as he saw me, the young man growled, and smoke rose from where he was sitting. It was like a Stephen King movie with the aid of Spielberg's special effects. I looked at him directly in the eye as I have done so many times with no fear whatsoever in me because I know he is empty. I commanded the devil to come out, and with no warning, fire ignited burning the sofa he was sitting on, I mean fire itself. I had seen the devil's antics before; however, I had not seen this manifestation at all. This was my first time dealing with such a case but definitely not my first time dealing with Jesus. I had revelation that the devil was empty of power and full of tricks. But one more thing I knew was the devil is a small entity. So I cast out that demon then got into my car and left.

Now too many Christians are caught up in what they call spiritual warfare where they spend hours in prayer fighting the devil. They are all over the place, from one all-night prayer service to another praying "warfare" prayers. They think the only time God can help them is at night. Do you realise when it's all night here, it's all day in New Zealand? There is no power in all-night prayer. And demons are not checking any clock anywhere to see what time of day it is.

This kind of spiritual warfare mentality is as ridiculous a notion as putting on a pair of boxing gloves to fight an ant! The devil is too small to fight. So, don't listen to these preachers who talk up the devil and tell you that you have to fight him. You don't! They are talking out of their own fear, and fear always makes things appear larger than they really are.

Deliverance *is* necessary, but only for those who don't know the Word. The ones who pray deliverance prayers and hold deliverance services need to be delivered from their ignorance. They need to understand that the only people who fight the devil are those who don't know we already defeated him in Christ. That fight is already won, so there's no need to continue fighting.

The devil is defeated, but he's a sore loser. So, when the fight ended, warfare continued, but not the way you think. No, we don't need to fight the devil, but we are engaged in warfare. So the question then becomes, how does something as little as the devil engage in warfare with us? First, you must understand the kind of warfare he is waging, the strategies he's employing. Because if you don't, although he is defeated, he will gain an advantage. The Bible says this in 2 Corinthians 2:11:

2 Corinthians 2:11
Lest Satan should get an advantage of us: for we are not ignorant of his devices.

Ignorance will get you taken advantage of. So, there is one more trick up the devil's sleeve that you need to know about if you are going to deal with him effectively.

Chapter Four

Jedi Mind Tricks

"And the Academy Award for Best Actor, Best Story, Best Adapted Screenplay, and Best Foreign Film goes to... the devil!"

Hollywood has played a big role in spiritual warfare, and the Church has rolled out the red carpet while the devil collects awards. Because of Hollywood, we now know that the devil wears Prada, runs a nightclub in Los Angeles (according to the television series *Lucifer*), and got into Rosemary's baby. We have seamlessly integrated the devil into our everyday vocabulary so that now we have become "devil's advocates," "make deals with the devil," and "give the devil his due." Hollywood has glamorised and elevated the devil to celebrity status, and the Church is busy taking selfies with Satan.

The Church has allowed Hollywood to define for us who the devil is, what he does, the power he has, even where he lives. Most Christians think demons are flying around, and the devil is coming out of hell. There is no Bible verse for that. The devil doesn't even want to see hell himself, neither are demons there.

The Bible tells us of a man in the country of the Gadarenes who was possessed by devils. He was a raving maniac, cutting himself with stones, and no man could bind him. The scripture tells us he was often bound with fetters and chains, but he would break them into pieces. He became so violent nobody could pass by that way until Jesus came.

This man was possessed by a legion of devils. A legion in the Roman army could be anywhere between 3,000 and 6,000 soldiers. Some believe a legion can be as many as 36,000. The point is, there were thousands of demons in this man. But I want you to notice that before Jesus even gave the command to kick them out, these demons—the same demons that had wreaked so much havoc and violence—suddenly became as weak as kittens and starting begging Jesus. They cried out *why are you tormenting us before the time?*

Mark 8:29
And, behold, they cried out, saying, What have we to do with thee, Jesus, thou Son of God? art thou come hither to torment us before the time?

They knew it was not yet time for them to be in hell. There is a set time for the devil and his cohorts to be in hell.

You see, most Christians have a contrived notion of how the devil operates. They've believed the image he helped to create that depicts him with a red cape, pitchfork, and the powers of a supervillain. One passage that immature preachers have used to tip the spiritual warfare scales in favour of the devil is in Matthew chapter 4 where Jesus is tempted in the wilderness by the devil.

The Bible tells us that the devil took Jesus up to the highest point of the temple in Jerusalem and dared Jesus to throw himself down from there to prove He was the Son of God. That's Matthew 4, verses 5 and 6:

Matthew 4:5-6
Then the devil taketh him up into the holy city, and setteth him on a pinnacle of the temple, And saith unto him, If thou be the Son of God, cast thyself down: for it is written, He shall give his angels charge concerning thee: and in their hands they shall bear thee up, lest at any time thou dash thy foot against a stone.

People read that passage and they think, *oh, the devil has a lot of power if he could transport Jesus to the top of the temple*. But it's not the way you think. This was not a physical thing. Remember, all the devil has is tricks.

In the *Star Wars* movie phenomenon, there was something introduced called the Jedi mind trick. It was the ability to influence someone's mind to the Jedi's advantage. An experienced Jedi could plant a suggestion in the minds of those they encountered, encouraging them to comply with the Jedi's wishes. The mind trick was said to work only on the weak-minded.

When the devil tempted Jesus, he did not have the power to physically take him anywhere. All he could do was try to use Jedi mind tricks to try to plant a thought in Jesus' mind. So when the Bible tells us that the devil took Jesus to the top of the temple and told Jesus to throw himself down, it was a *thought* that the devil planted in Jesus' mind. But "Jedi mind tricks" only work on the weak-minded, those who do not know the Word.

I know some of you are still struggling because you still believe the devil had to have some kind of power to plant a thought in the mind of Jesus. But you're mistaken. Anyone can plant a thought in the mind of another person with one simple mechanism, *words*. The devil did not plant a thought in Jesus' mind by osmosis. He spoke. For the devil to suggest that Jesus should cast himself down from the pinnacle of the temple, he first had to plant the imagery of the temple in Jesus' mind. And the only way he could do that is with words.

It doesn't take any special power to plant a thought in someone's mind. If I say the word "yellow" to you, your mind immediately creates a corresponding correlation to the colour yellow. Even a child can do that. There was no power involved in the devil planting that thought in Jesus' mind.

Remember, it was the Holy Ghost who led Jesus into the wilderness *for the purpose of* being tempted by the devil. The keyword there is *tempted*. There is no sin in being tempted. And weakness is not determined by temptation, but by succumbing to it. Jesus was not, by any definition of the word, weak. He never succumbed to any temptation. The Bible lets us know that He was tempted in every possible way, yet without sin.

Hebrews 4:15
For we have not an high priest which cannot be touched with the feeling of our infirmities; but *was in all points tempted like as we are, yet without sin* [emphasis added].

Jesus was sent into the wilderness to be tempted, not to show how weak He was, but to demonstrate the power to resist and repel the enemy.

Notice how Jesus responded to the "Jedi mind trick" of the devil. He used the Word. This is what you need to understand when the devil tries to pull his Jedi mind tricks on you. The Bible says the devil goes around *like* a roaring lion seeking whom he may devour. That's a verse that strikes terror in a lot of Christians hearts and drives them into frenzied warfare prayers. But that should not be your response at all. Our response to the devil's going about like a roaring lion is only to be aware of his tricks. Watch what the Bible says in 1 Peter 5, verses 8 and 9:

1 Peter 5:8-9
Be sober, be vigilant; because your adversary the devil, as a roaring lion, walketh about, seeking whom he may devour: Whom resist stedfast in the faith, knowing that the same afflictions are accomplished in your brethren that are in the world.

Do you see anywhere in those verses that tell you that when the devil goes about like a roaring lion you should be fighting? Where in there do you see anything about doing warfare? It's not there. This is an exposé of one of the devil's tricks. Most Christians miss it, yet it's right there in the verse. Notice, it says the devil goes around "as" or *like* a roaring lion. It did not say the devil is a roaring lion; it says he tries to act *like* one.

In grammar, there is something called a simile. A simile is a figure of speech involving the comparison of one thing with another thing *of a different kind*. So, whenever you hear "like" or "as," that means the thing being described as "like" or "as" is different from the thing to which it is being compared. That lets you know right there that if the devil is going around *as* a roaring lion, he is *not* a roaring lion. When you go into warfare to fight against the devil as a roaring lion, you are shadowboxing an imaginary opponent who has led you to believe he is bigger than what he really is.

Jesus knew He is the Lion; the devil was only roaring, pretending to be something he is not. So Jesus responded the way every Christian should respond: He showed the devil who the real Lion is, and He roared back. Brother and sisters, when the devil roars at you trying to intimidate you or tempt you to move from your position of victory, all you need to do is *roar back*!

Let's go back to Matthew chapter 4 to see this kind of roaring in action. Let's pick it up from verses 8 and 9:

Matthew 4:8-9
8 Again, the devil taketh him up into an exceeding high mountain, and sheweth him all the kingdoms of the world, and the glory of them; 9 And saith unto him, All these things will I give thee, if thou wilt fall down and worship me.

Now, when you read verse 8, you should understand that this again was an attempted Jedi mind trick of the devil and not a physical thing. What I want you to see is how Jesus responded in verse 10:

Matthew 4:10
Then saith Jesus unto him, Get thee hence, Satan: for it is written, Thou shalt worship the Lord thy God, and him only shalt thou serve.

It says, "then *saith* Jesus unto him." If you go back and look at verse 7, you will see Jesus gave a similar response when the devil planted the thought about Jesus throwing himself down from the top of the temple. Notice I said *similar*. In verse 7, Jesus responded, "**it is written**," and the devil didn't leave. As a matter of fact, the devil came right back with another attempted Jedi mind trick which we read in verses 8 and 9. But this time, Jesus responds with, "**it is said**." And what happened? The devil left.

What made the difference? Jesus said man lives not by the written word but by the spoken word that comes from the mouth of God. Matthew 4, verse 4 says:

Matthew 4:4
But he answered and said, It is written, Man shall not live by bread alone, but by every word that proceedeth out of the mouth of God.

When Jesus stopped quoting the written word and got into the *rhema* spoken word, that's when the devil left.

Matthew 4:11
Then the devil leaveth him, and, behold, angels came and ministered unto him.

Quiet Christians die quietly. Christianity is for talkers. You can't be quiet while the devil is roaring at you with Jedi mind tricks. 1 Peter 5 tells us how to respond—we must *resist*.

1 Peter 5:9
Whom resist stedfast in the faith...

How do you resist? It says, "in the faith." That does not mean that you remain quiet, and inside you say you have faith. No! Faith is for talkers! The Bible says the spirit of faith speaks! 2 Corinthians 4, verse 13 says it this way:

2 Corinthians 4:13
We having the same spirit of faith, according as it is written, I believed, and therefore have I spoken; we also believe, and therefore speak;

Understand the strategies of the devil's trickery. The devil doesn't have any power except the power that you give to him. His scheme is to plant a thought in your mind making use of the power of your own imagination.

This is not a physical thing. That's why the Bible tells us:

2 Corinthians 10:3
For though we walk in the flesh, we do not war after the flesh:

That means your resistance is also not physical. Watch what 2 Corinthians 10, verses 4 and 5 says:

2 Corinthians 10:4-5
(For the weapons of our warfare are not carnal, but mighty through God to the pulling down of strong holds;) Casting down imaginations, and every high thing that exalteth itself against the knowledge of God, and bringing into captivity every thought to the obedience of Christ

The immature Christian will read those verses, and it's as though someone took a fluorescent marker and highlighted the word "warfare." That's all they see, and they use that as fuel for their warfare prayer points. This is not about warfare or prayer points. This is a statement of victory! The Holy Ghost is telling you that you have weapons and these weapons are mighty through God. But they are not for fighting. It says these weapons are for "pulling down strongholds" and "casting down imaginations." Pulling and casting is not fighting. These are not physical strongholds; this is talking about the mind.

The devil is an old adversary, and so are his tricks. He uses the same tricks he used on Jesus during the temptation in the wilderness. So you don't have to reinvent the wheel and try to come up with a new way to "fight" the devil, no! All you need to do is employ the same successful strategy that Jesus used. When the enemy tries his tricks to plant a thought in your mind and to use the power of your own imagination against you, your response should be the rhema of God.

Only words can defeat other words. When an evil word is spoken, you have the power to speak a greater word to neutralise that evil word. The prophet Isaiah put it like this:

Isaiah 54:17
No weapon that is formed against thee shall prosper; and every tongue that shall rise against thee in judgment thou shalt condemn.

When words are spoken, you must also respond with words. That is how you pull down strongholds.

A stronghold is a fortification. It's something you uphold. So when the devil speaks a lie, it's an attempt to get you to believe it. If you believe it, you *uphold* his opinion in your mind. So the Bible says refuse to uphold the lie of the devil. When he tries to erect a lie in your mind, pull it down! This is not a passive rejection. You need to be actively speaking the Word of God.

Let me drop one more point in here before we close this chapter. You cannot discern a lie unless you know the truth. And this is exactly why immature Christians waste their energy fighting the devil. They don't have the knowledge of the truth. Every person who is skilled in detecting counterfeit money is trained by studying the real thing. They know how real money looks, feels, and smells. They know what's printed on it and exactly what to look for. They become so familiar with the real thing that as soon as a counterfeit shows up, they can recognise it.

The Bible tells us that we must cast down imaginations *and* every high thing that exalts itself above the *knowledge of God*. The only way you can recognise when the devil is trying to mount a counterfeit thought or imagination in your mind is to already have the knowledge of God. You need the Word. The difference between you fighting the devil in spiritual warfare and maintaining the victory Christ has already secured for you is the amount of Word in you.

Chapter Five

The Skinny on Spiritual Warfare

In October of 2015, a twenty-something entrepreneur from Sand City, California entered the Shark Tank studio. She stood, palms sweating and heart racing, in front of five of the most ferocious titans in the business industry. She was there to pitch her new product seeking an investment of $200,000 in exchange for 20% equity in her company. It was an audacious million-dollar valuation of an unpatented product that she believed would change everything about the way you see yourself. It was called the Skinny Mirror.

She was all smiles, making her pitch with great enthusiasm, giving convincing arguments about retailers increasing clothing sales by eighteen per cent. She seemed certain that her product was the next best thing to sliced bread. An offer would soon be on the table. At least that's what she thought. But Kevin "Mr Wonderful" O'Leary, didn't think her product was so wonderful. He abruptly ended her pitch and dismissed her product as a sham, snake oil in a 16 x 48-inch frame. There was nothing new about the Skinny Mirror. It is the repackaging of an age-old trick the devil has been using to keep immature Christians engaged in spiritual warfare. It is the ultimate deception.

You see, the Skinny Mirror is designed to present you with an image of yourself that isn't true, a skinnier version. It makes you look ten pounds slimmer than you really are. It's a feel-good tactic. This is what the devil does. He shows you a version of yourself that makes you feel good. The problem is the version that makes the immature Christian feel good is the one that shows them that they need to be delivered.

The immature Christian wants to see themselves as victimised by the devil. They want to blame him for every misfortune that happens in their life. They would rather look into that mirror and believe they have a demon that is causing their sickness, poverty, and pain. So, they look into the devil's Skinny Mirror which shows them just what they want to see. Then they run, not walk, to the nearest available deliverance service. Do they need deliverance? Yes, they do but only because they have believed the lie of the devil.

Proverbs 23, verse 7 says it this way:

Proverbs 23: 7
For as he thinketh in his heart, so is he: Eat and drink, saith he to thee; but his heart is not with thee.

That simply means that you will act like who you believe yourself to be. That is the concept behind the Skinny Mirror. But if who you believe yourself to be is based on a false idea, you have a big problem. This is what Christians who are fighting the devil in spiritual warfare fail to understand.

In Galatians chapter 4, verse 1, the Bible says, the heir as long as he is a child will never enjoy the benefits of his inheritance.

Galatians 4:1
Now I say, That the heir, as long as he is a child, differeth nothing from a servant, though he be lord of all

As long as the heir sees himself or herself as a child, that's how they'll act. Yet the Bible says everything is already yours. But if you're not mature enough to realise that, you will be ruled by the one you should be ruling over, namely the devil.

There is a verse that typifies that dilemma which puzzled even the brilliant mind of one of the wisest men on earth, Solomon. Look at what he says in Ecclesiastes chapter 10, verse 7:

Ecclesiastes 10:7
I have seen servants [slaves] upon horses, and princes walking as servants upon the earth.

This is an error! The false image that you see in the devil's mirror leads you to believe that you are something you're not, which in turn makes you careless.

Take the Skinny Mirror, for example. When you look in that mirror and see yourself as 120 pounds, but you are really 170 pounds, you will become careless with your diet and exercise. Why? Because, according to the mirror, you don't need to pay attention to your diet. That is the tactic the devil uses to make immature Christians vulnerable in spiritual warfare. He holds up his version of the Skinny Mirror so that you become careless with your spiritual diet.

Feed Your Spirit

You need to understand that your spirit man, the real you, feeds on the Word of God just as your physical body feeds on natural food. It is essential to feed your spirit every day with the Word of God. If you feed your body three hot meals a day and your spirit only one cold snack a week, you will definitely need deliverance. The devil will fight you and win.

The pitch for the Skinny Mirror is also its downfall—not all mirrors are created equal. The creator of the Skinny Mirror overlooked one major flaw: you have to ignore every other mirror in order to maintain the same deceptive image. The devil doesn't want you to look at any mirror other than the one he's holding in front of you because he's afraid that you will see yourself as you truly are. But in order to grasp the reality of who you really are, you need to look at a different mirror, which is the Word of God. 2 Corinthians 3, verse 18 says:

2 Corinthians 3: 18
But we all, with open face beholding as in a glass the glory of the Lord, are changed into the same image from glory to glory, *even* as by the Spirit of the Lord.

The scriptures tell us that the Word of God is a mirror. It shows you who you are. But not only that, it shows you who you are becoming. In Ephesians chapter 5, Paul tells us that we are members of His body, of His flesh, and of His bones!

Ephesians 5:30
For we are members of his body, of his flesh, and of his bones.

I don't know if that scripture excites you the way it excites me. When I read a verse like that, I get turned on in my spirit! It's telling us that we are members, *body parts* of Christ. Oh, glory be to Jesus! You think you are something small, but you are the walking, talking body parts of Jesus. You are Jesus in your house, Jesus on your job, Jesus wherever you are!

I know some of you childish Christians will have a problem with me saying that, but that doesn't make it any less true. Immature Christians easily believe worldly sayings, but they stumble when it comes to the Word of God. If I tell you the common saying, "you are what you eat," you wouldn't have a problem with that. But when I tell you that you are the body parts of Jesus, you baulk at the truth, yet the principle is the same. When you consume the Word, you become the Word.

No wonder Paul exclaimed in Galatians 4:19, I travail to see Christ fully formed in you.

Galatians 4:19
My little children, of whom I travail in birth again until Christ be formed in you,

Paul is saying, Christ is being fully formed in you, but you won't see that unless you are looking at, feeding on, gazing into the mirror of the Word.

The Bible says as many as have put on Christ are baptised into Christ. That's Galatians 3, verses 26 and 27.

Galatians 3:26-27
For ye are all the children of God by faith in Christ Jesus. For as many of you as have been baptised into Christ have put on Christ.

So, we are baptised into Christ. The word baptised comes from the Greek word *baptízō* which means *to immerse, to submerge*. When we are baptised into Christ, we sink down into Him, but Christ is not baptised into us.

Let me illustrate it this way. I can take a glass of water and drop some sugar cubes in there. The moment I drop the cubes in there, they are *baptised* into the water—fully immersed—and they begin to dissolve. *But,* as long as you still see granules of sugar, it has not been completely taken over by the water. So, although the sugar is baptised into the water, the water is not fully in the sugar.

Now, using that same illustration, Christ is the water, and you are the sugar cube. You are baptised into Christ. The water entering the sugar is symbolic of the Word entering you. And remember, Christ is the Word. So, the only way Christ can be fully formed, baptised into you, is through reading and hearing the Word of God.

Fighting the devil in spiritual warfare happens because there's still too much sugar in the water and not enough water in the sugar. As Paul continues from the verse we read earlier in Galatians 4:1, you are still a child. Christ is not fully formed in you. As a result, you are held in bondage to the elements of this world.

Galatians 4:1, 3
Now I say, That the heir, as long as he is a child, differeth nothing from a servant, though he be lord of all;

Even so we, when we were children, were in bondage under the elements of the world:

Paul is telling us precisely who needs deliverance. It is the childish Christian who is in bondage to the *elements*—the *stoicheîon*—the elementary things of this world. Without the Word in you, small-small things will put you in bondage. And the devil is a small-small thing.

Watch what the Bible says in the book of Hebrews chapter 5, verses 12 and 13:

Hebrews 5:12-13
For when for the time ye ought to be teachers, ye have need that one teach you again which be the first principles of the oracles of God; and are become such as have need of milk, and not of strong meat. For every one that useth milk is unskilful in the word of righteousness: for he is a babe.

Paul calls those who are unskilful in the Word of righteousness babes in Christ. The Greek word translated as unskilful in that passage is *apeiros*, and it literally means ignorant. So then, those who are ignorant of the Word of righteousness are the *nepios*, the babes in Christ, still needing deliverance fifteen years after receiving Christ.

A *nepios* is someone who doesn't know how to talk. A babe in Christ lacks the spiritual vocabulary that is required to maintain a position of victory. The Word of God is talking material. It gives you what to say. The problem with you is when you look in the mirror all you see is a reflective surface. But when I look in the mirror, I have talking sessions! Because when I look in the mirror, Christ in me sees himself and starts talking about what He sees. Why? Because I've been looking at Him all this while. And as I gaze at Him through the Word of God, I am *metamorphóō—transformed* into His image. Paul says it this way:

2 Corinthians 3:18
But we all, with open face beholding as in a glass the glory of the Lord, are changed into the same image from glory to glory, even as by the Spirit of the Lord.

We are changed as we look into the mirror of the Word of God and keep looking.

The devil doesn't want you to look at the mirror of the Word. You see, he is running his own "only believe" campaign. With all his shenanigans, he has one focus, one goal, and that is to convince you to believe his lies. It's like you looking at the Word, then you look at the devil's mirror, and you forget what you saw in the Word. James says it this way:

James 1:23-24
For if any be a hearer of the word, and not a doer, he is like unto a man beholding his natural face in a glass: For he beholdeth himself, and goeth his way, and straightway forgetteth what manner of man he was.

That's what immature Christians do. They forget what the Word says. Do they need deliverance when that happens? Yes! But preachers won't tell them the truth. The deliverance they need comes by looking into the mirror of God's Word. But because you are immature, you require the preacher to cast out your demons.

Some preachers will gladly oblige. They'll even charge you nicely for that service. Five hundred dollars to cast out the demon of poverty. If a demon of poverty entered for free, why should you pay five hundred dollars to get it cast out! But you have looked into the devil's skinny mirror, and now all you see are demons looking back at you. Listen, demons come quietly. They can also leave quietly. As the Word is being ministered, demons are checking out. But you won't believe unless you roll on the floor and vomit.

In John chapter 8, Jesus met a woman who had demons. The Bible says she was caught in the act of adultery and dragged to Jesus. There she was, right in front of the mirror of the Word, surrounded by men who were all holding the devil's mirrors showing her demons. When she encountered Jesus, who is the Word, something remarkable happened. She looked away from the devil's mirror and looked at the mirror of the Word. The Word spoke to her and said, "**go, and sin no more**." She did not roll on the ground or foam at the mouth. She came to the Word with demons and left with the empowerment to resist the devil.

Brothers and sisters, the Word of God is the ultimate and authentic Skinny Mirror. It not only shows you who you are, but it has the power to make you become what it shows you. But for that to happen, you must be looking at the Word. Remove your eyes from every other thing and focus on the Word. Refuse to be careless about your spiritual diet and exercise. Feed your spirit with the Word. And don't just look at it, start talking it, keep saying it. As you do these things, you will see who you really are in Christ, and you will refuse to fight with someone as insignificant as the devil.

Chapter Six

The Influence of the Mind

MythBusters, the former Australian-American science entertainment television program, set out to debunk the myth that Chinese water torture could drive someone insane. Psychotherapist Dr Gerald Gray, an expert in counselling thousands of torture victims, explains the torture process. A prisoner is immobilized, and slow drips of water are dropped onto one small area of their forehead for long durations. The forehead, being one of the most sensitive parts of the body, was found to be the most suitable point for this form of torture.

Could tiny little drops of water on a localized area become a powerful persuader? That was the question the experiment set out to answer, and a question that bears great significance in the issue of spiritual warfare.

Two brave volunteers, Kari and Adam, would be the subjects. The experiment would be carried out in tandem with one varying factor. Kari would be bound in restraints, but Adam would not. A torture chamber was rigged to secure Kari. Her head would be placed in a brace to keep it still, with a constantly dripping tap above it. Both subjects started the experiment in good spirits knowing they could stop it at any time.

The camera zooms in on Kari as the paramedic checks her vital signs. Before the experiment begins, she's asked a set of questions to establish her stress levels.

"Do you feel nervous and anxious?"
She smiles. "Sometimes."
"Have you ever felt afraid?"
She smiles again, but this time as though the question caught her off guard. "Sometimes."

As Kari is stretched out on the wooden rack and shackled hands and feet, she reminds herself that this is not real. She can call this off at any time, and the shackles can be removed within seconds. They start the clock, and the torture begins. One drop after the other, every two seconds, a cold drop of water strikes Kari's forehead in exactly the same spot, every time.

At first, she finds the drips somewhat annoying. Fifteen minutes into it, she's surprised she's been able to withstand the torture that long. She's asked the same questions she was asked before the torture began.

"Do you feel nervous or anxious?"
"Mild," she responds.
"Do you feel afraid?"
"Mild."
"How easily would you get upset right now?"
"Easily."

Kari thinks she's holding up relatively well. But the power of water torture is meant to increase the longer it goes on. After an hour on the rack, Kari's face is noticeably tensed. Her eyes stare straight ahead as if she thinks she can make herself invincible by sheer force of will. Her vital signs are still within the safe range, but the torture is starting to tell on her emotions. Again, she's asked the same questions.

"Do you feel nervous and anxious?"
"Yes."
"Would you say mild, moderate or severe?"
"Severe."
"Are you afraid?"
She responds in the negative, but as she answers a tear escapes and rolls down the side of her face.
"Are you getting upset or feel like you're going to panic?"
"Yes. Extreme panic."

And she breaks into a weep. After a few moments, she regains her composure, but it's not fun anymore. The line between experiment and reality has blurred. Later, she describes that moment as sheer terror and panic. Even though she knew she could get up at any time, the feeling of being bound overwhelmed her senses, and she "freaked out."

Adam lasted three whole hours and was more annoyed by a pesky fly than the dripping water. He knew he was not bound, so the supposed torture was rendered ineffective. Kari managed to last an hour and a half before the paramedic, alarmed by her psychological and physical distress, stopped the experiment. Even though she knew she could stop the torture at any time, the restraints threw her into sheer panic. She summed up her experience in one simple phrase, "being bound is crazy."

The devil is a plumber's nightmare. His constant drip of insidious thoughts drives the weak-minded to the brink of spiritual insanity. He is persistent in the worst sense of the word. But that is not what defeats the immature Christian. It is their own persistent thoughts that they are bound that throws them into sheer panic and sends them gasping for deliverance from demons. They fail to recognize that Jesus removed the torture rack and shackles long ago. But because their minds are convinced that they are bound, they suffer the most tortuous effects.

Understand where warfare takes place. It happens in the mind just as it did when Jesus was tempted in the wilderness. This idea you have of Jesus and the devil having a physical confrontation in the wilderness is absurd. The temptation of Jesus was not a physical thing. The devil had no power to take Jesus anywhere physically. It was an assault on the mind of Jesus. The devil is a spirit, only Jesus was in the flesh. So, the only way the devil could interact with Jesus was to try to infiltrate His mind with his own devilish thoughts.

This is the modus operandi of the devil. He seeks to influence your mind. His strategy is to try to give you a way of thinking—a mentality, or as is seen most times in churches, he uses doctrines. And he uses tricks. The devil will never plant a thought of suicide and say, *you want to kill yourself*. Instead, he speaks in the first person and plants the thought, "*I* want to kill *myself*." He makes you think it's your own idea, your own thoughts. He is notorious for employing a Chinese water torture technique. He aims his lies at your head because it is your mind that he wants to capture. But he can only do that if you already think that you are bound.

When the Bible speaks of pulling down strongholds, people think they are pulling down demons who are persistent when it's *thoughts* that are persistent. That's why we ought to be casting down *imaginations*. Look at what the scripture says in 2 Corinthians chapter 10, verses 4 and 5:

2 Corinthians 10:4-5a
(For the weapons of our warfare are not carnal, but mighty through God to the pulling down of strong holds;) *Casting down imaginations* **[emphasis added]**

'Imagination' is the Greek word *logismós*, which means *reasoning, imagination, a thought.* An imagination is a thought that you hold in place in your mind, the way you frame a picture so you can look at it. The devil plants evil imaginations in the mind in hopes that you'll hold it there by believing his lies.

When a Christian believes he is possessed, that's an evil imagination that he failed to cast down. The Christian cannot be possessed by the devil. He or she is already possessed by the Holy Ghost. What the devil does is to try to exert external influence on the mind. In other words, he is outside of you, attempting to influence your mind. He wants you to frame the wrong thoughts and uphold them in your mind.

One of the biggest problems in the Church is that there are too many Christians holding the wrong thoughts in their minds. They are carnally minded, and the Bible tells us that the carnal mind is at *enmity* with God.

Romans 8:7
Because the carnal mind is enmity against God: for it is not subject to the law of God, neither indeed can be.

The carnal mind is the residence of the devil's strongholds. Filled with worldly knowledge rather than the Word, it is a gallery where the lies of the devil are framed and placed on exhibit. And people are dying because they have framed the wrong thing in their minds.

Have you ever wondered why we seldom hear of doctors diagnosing cancer at stage 1 or 2? It's because the person endorses stage 3 or 4 in their mind when they get the diagnosis. The doctor tells them that they have three weeks to live, so they frame that picture in their mind. They believe the lie that the devil put cancer in them, and they imagine themselves dying. Why is it that the three-week clock only starts ticking the moment they get the diagnosis? They have too much knowledge of the things of the world but not enough knowledge of the Word. So, they believe they are powerless, immobilized on the rack, and that belief is what defeats them. That is why they need deliverance.

The devil wants you to believe he can give you a disease. He cannot. He can only try to trick you into thinking you have the symptoms of a disease, but you have to agree that the symptoms are a disease. It is that endorsement of a disease that gives you the disease. Your endorsement of the symptoms gives the disease a hold. Don't agree or endorse symptoms. Be saturated by the Word. Everything about you—including and especially your mind—must be saturated by the Word.

Christ sinks into you by a certain revelation. Like sugar that is completely dissolved in water, there should be no space in you that is not affected by God. You ought to get to a point where you are convinced, because of the Word in you, that you can never be possessed by a demon. To be possessed means to be taken over entirely. That is not possible while Christ is in you. But the part that is not completely taken over by Christ can be *affected* by a demon. But understand, it's all about the mind.

When the devil wants to destroy you, he uses you to destroy yourself. He gets into your mind and starts from there. That's all he does is plays tricks with people's minds. Like the woman in the experiment discovered, it wasn't the constant drip of water that drove her to the brink of psychological breakdown. It was her believing that she was bound and helpless that defeated her. Her own thoughts worked against her. That's the strategy the devil uses in spiritual warfare. He tries to trick you into thinking that he has you bound, and it is that bondage mindset that has the most tortuous effect. It leads you to believe you are restrained, but you can decide to leave that position at any time.

Brothers and sisters, the devil is experimenting with your mind. He's testing to see if his persistent lies can persuade you. But you can stop him at any time. Martin Luther said, "You cannot keep birds from flying over your head, but you can keep them from building a nest in your hair." You don't need the man of God to give you a miracle. You can give yourself one. The devil may drip his lies, but you can choose to move your head out from under his leaky faucet and get under the flow of the water of the Word. Join in on the woman's conclusion after the Chinese water torture experiment ended and be convinced that "being bound is crazy!"

One day I was faced face to face with a voodoo black magic priest. The whole neighbourhood knew his fits and how he could transform himself into unspeakable things. He would deceive people with demonic feats and exploits. Everyone feared him, and many went to him for help. The funny part is we had gone to the same primary school when I was but a little boy, so he had also heard of my power in the Lord. The moment I touched down, he seemed to have gotten wind of my arrival. He came there fired up in front of my team and my first-born son.

He hurled insults towards me and towards Jesus Christ, calling me powerless and Christ useless. When it was all about me, I did give him any notice until he mentioned my Lord and Saviour. You see, in my area, people gather for anything, and we seemed to attract a lot of unwanted audiences. But they were in for a treat.

I immediately told him, "Stand in front of me if you are really a man of power as you suppose." He quickly responded by standing there in front of me, something I never imagined he would agree to. At that moment, I called the name of Jesus and declared, "In the name of Jesus, may the power that is less bow before the mightier one, in the name of Jesus."

With that, his knees buckled, and to the joy of many, one hit the ground. Before the other reached the ground, he sprung into an escape. He ran with everyone clapping their hands, celebrating the ever so powerful name of Jesus. The black magic priest stood from afar shaking his head in amazement wondering what power I was using. You see, I have seen too much. The devil has no power. He is so empty that if Christians knew it, they would kick him out every time.

Chapter Seven

When Deliverance Is Needed

There is a hunter who sets out to catch a monkey in the forest. The hunter is unarmed, and the monkey is out of reach, far above him in the treetops. The hunter knows the only way it can catch the monkey is to use a trick. So he gets a coconut and cuts two holes in it, one large enough for a piece of rope to thread through, and the other just large enough for the monkey's open hand to fit. Then he puts some nuts inside the coconut as bait, threads some rope through the holes and fastens the coconut to the base of the tree. After setting his trap, the hunter moves out of sight and watches.

The monkey climbs down out of the tree and reaches his hand inside the coconut. It grabs a fistful of nuts and attempts to remove his hand, not realising that as long as his hand is balled up in a fist, it will never fit through the hole. He's stuck. He fights and fights to free himself, but the more he holds on to the nuts, the more stuck he remains. As the unarmed hunter moves in on his prey, the monkey fights even harder to hold on to what he has. The hunter relies on the stupidity of the monkey, knowing it will choose to fight when all it needs to do is let go of what is in its hand. Without the hunter using a single weapon, the monkey is easily caught because of his own unwillingness to let go of what he believes belongs to him. That is an accurate depiction of spiritual warfare.

Hunters use this strategy to catch all kinds and sizes of monkeys from Pygmy Marmosets to Mandrills. The devil also employs the same strategy to entangle Christians in warfare, from new converts to archbishops. Its effectiveness is due to one simple susceptibility, and that is the desire many Christians have for ownership.

"Mine" is the most dangerous word in the Christian's vocabulary. It is the "mine" mindset that causes Christians to get caught up in fighting a weaponless devil. It brings you down to his base level, which is the only way he can get access to you. Ownership is a liability that causes casualties in spiritual warfare. It gives the devil access. That was the lesson Potiphar learned the hard way.

Potiphar was an Egyptian ruler who had the good fortune of having Joseph enter his household. Joseph entered Potiphar's household as a servant, but the Bible tells us that the Lord was with Joseph, and he was a prosperous man. You'll find that in Genesis chapter 39, verse 2:

Genesis 39:2
And the Lord was with Joseph, and he was a prosperous man; and he was in the house of his master the Egyptian.

Now, Potiphar began to notice that ever since Joseph came to his house, there was a noticeable improvement in his affairs. So much so, the Bible says Potiphar *saw* that the Lord was with Joseph. So he put Joseph in charge over everything he had in his house and in the field. Now, I want you to look closely at what the Bible says in Genesis 39, verses 3 through 5:

Genesis 39:3-5

And his master saw that the Lord was with him, and that the Lord made all that he did to prosper in his hand. And Joseph found grace in his sight, and he served him: and he made him overseer over his house, and all that he had he put into his hand. And it came to pass from the time that he had made him overseer in his house, and over all that he had, that the Lord blessed the Egyptian's house for Joseph's sake; and the blessing of the Lord was upon all that he had in the house, and in the field.

Notice that the Bible tells us that the blessing of the Lord was on everything that was under Joseph's care. That's where Potiphar messed up. Let's look at the text to see what happened.

Genesis 39:6-10

And he left all that he had in Joseph's hand; and he knew not ought he had, save the bread which he did eat. And Joseph was a goodly person, and well favoured. And it came to pass after these things, that his master's wife cast her eyes upon Joseph; and she said, Lie with me. But he refused, and said unto his master's wife, Behold, my master wotteth not what is with me in the house, and he hath committed all that he hath to my hand; There is none greater in this house than I; *neither hath he kept back any thing from me but thee* [emphasis added], because thou art his wife: how then can I do this great wickedness, and sin against God? And it came to pass, as she spake to Joseph day by day, that he hearkened not unto her, to lie by her, or to be with her.

Potiphar put everything in his household under Joseph's care except his wife. He said, in effect, she is *mine*. And the thing he kept as "mine" is the thing through which the devil came, and so his wife became obsessed with seducing Joseph. You see, whatever you don't fully submit to God becomes the area the devil will use to get into your life.

The devil gained access through the one area of Potiphar's life that was not under Joseph's—and consequently, God's—control. As a result, Potiphar's wife joined the Me Too movement: Joseph was accused of sexual harassment and thrown in prison; Potiphar lost the blessings he had because of Joseph's sake, and the devil was laughing the whole time. If Potiphar had just released that nut (his wife) into Joseph's care, he would have continued enjoying the blessings of God with no interference from the devil.

Submit to Christ Through the Word

Anything you don't submit to Jesus fully through the Word and its power to transform your mindset will give access to the devil. And whenever you give access to the devil, that is when warfare is needed. The devil can't touch anything that belongs to Christ. Your submission to the Word establishes His ownership.

You need to understand that there is a difference between ownership and stewardship. If you understand the Bible, you will realise that you own nothing, yet you are the steward of everything God has blessed you with. A steward is a manager of someone else's assets and resources. The Bible says that every good thing comes from God (see James 1:17), and God turns those things over to you. That's why the Bible says, "all things are yours."

1 Corinthians 3:21
Therefore let no man glory in men. For all things are yours.

You are the steward of your health, prosperity, children, marriage, and every other good thing with which God has blessed you. When you put everything in your life in submission to the Word of God, you turn everything back over to Him and say *you're the Owner, I'm the manager.* That means you don't have to fight the devil to protect anything. God protects and blesses what belongs to Him and insures it against any loss.

Too many Christians are unwilling to let go of what they believe belongs to them. They are ignorant of the privileges that they have because they haven't checked what the Word says. Their ownership becomes their liability because they think they have to protect what they own. That is why they fight with the devil. But look at what the devil himself declared as is recorded in Job chapter 1:

Job 1:9-10
Then Satan answered the Lord, and said, Doth Job fear God for nought? Hast not thou made an hedge about him, and about his house, and about all that he hath on every side? thou hast blessed the work of his hands, and his substance is increased in the land.

Did you catch that? He said there's a hedge around Job, around his house, and around everything he has on every side! How do you suppose the devil knew the hedge was there? There's only one way. He tried to get access to Job, his household, all that he had, and by his own admission, he checked every side, and there was no way in.

Now, remember we're talking about Job, an Old Testament personality. You also need to remember that the devil was saying this before Jesus came and stripped him of his power. Even then he recognised that Job was untouchable. Oh, glory be to God! I'm rejoicing because you're about to understand exactly who you are. And when you do, your days of fighting the devil will be over!

Now, watch this. Job did not have the assurance of the victorious indwelling Christ. Yet, he was protected to the point where the devil couldn't find an inch of access to anything concerning him. His blessings were secure, out of the reach of the devil. Do you think that Christ died to give you less than what Job had? No, a thousand times, no! Watch what the Bible says in Ephesians 1:3:

Ephesians 1:3
Blessed be the God and Father of our Lord Jesus Christ, who hath blessed us with all spiritual blessings in heavenly places in Christ.

That verse is telling us that we have blessings that are superior to anything Job or Joseph had or any blessing Potiphar experienced. We read that because of Joseph, who is a type or symbol of Christ, the blessings came *upon* Potiphar's house and field and everything that was under Joseph's care.

Genesis 39:5
And it came to pass from the time that he had made him overseer in his house, and over all that he had, that the Lord

blessed the Egyptian's house for Joseph's sake; *and the blessing of the Lord was upon all that he had in the house, and in the field* **[emphasis added].**

Job and Potiphar had blessings *upon*, but we have blessings *in* Christ, a place that is unreachable to the devil. The only way the devil can get to you is if you believe his lies. Doing so will move you away from the place of complete invincibility that you have in Christ and bring you down to the devil's level.

Do you understand what it means to be in Christ? You are out of the devil's reach. This is something that Apostle Paul desperately wanted us to understand. Ephesians 1, verses 18 through 23 says it this way:

Ephesians 1:18-21
The eyes of your understanding being enlightened; that ye may know what is the hope of his calling, and what the riches of the glory of his inheritance in the saints, And what is the exceeding greatness of his power to us-ward who believe, according to the working of his mighty power, Which he wrought in Christ, when he raised him from the dead, and set him at his own right hand in the heavenly places, Far above all principality, and power, and might, and dominion, and every name that is named, not only in this world, but also in that which is to come: And hath put all things under his feet, and gave him to be the head over all things to the church, Which is his body, the fulness of him that filleth all in all.

Paul is telling us where Christ is—His heavenly position and power—so that you can understand what he means when he says, you are *in* Christ. Christ is seated, not just above but *far above all* (not some) principality and power and might and dominion. If that's where Christ is, that's where you are. It goes on to say, all things are under His feet. That's where the devil is. And if he's under Christ's feet, since you are in Christ, the devil is under your feet. And just in case you don't get it in chapter 1, he continues in chapter 2:

Ephesians 2:6
And hath raised us up together, and made us sit together in heavenly places in Christ Jesus [emphasis added].

Brother, sister, everything that is true about Christ is true about you. If the devil can't touch Christ (and he can't), he can't touch you. You are seated in heavenly places *in Christ*.

Jesus, even before His victory over the devil, declared that there was nothing in Him to which the devil had access. Look at what it says in John chapter 14, verse 30:

John 14:30
Hereafter I will not talk much with you: for the prince of this world cometh, and hath nothing in me.

Jesus was untouchable even before He died on the cross. There was nothing in Him that the devil could find that would give him access. Jesus' mind was full of the scriptures, and He was set on the course that He had to follow. He knew exactly who He was and what He came to do. When He died on the cross, went down to Hell and whooped the devil on his own turf, he did that as a man. When He rose triumphantly from the grave, He took His place of authority and invincible power. And when He arose, the Bible says, we arose with Him. Romans chapter 6 says it this way:

Romans 6:3-4
Know ye not, that so many of us as were baptised into Jesus Christ were baptised into his death? Therefore we are buried with him by baptism into death: that like as Christ was raised up from the dead by the glory of the Father, even so we also should walk in newness of life.

There is nothing weak or vulnerable about you. You are in Christ, a place of invincibility, seated far above principalities and powers. Do you understand? You are invincible, unkillable!

This has to be your mindset. Otherwise, when the devil whispers his lies, you will be like the monkey who was out of reach of the hunter but came down and grabbed a fistful of the devil's bait. Understand that what the devil said about Job is a thousand times truer for you. You are in Christ, heavily protected, heavily guarded, and heavily defended. And everything you submit to the Word of God is brought under Christ's dominion. The only time the devil can get access to you or what belongs to you is if you replace that submission with your ownership.

My wife and I live in a mansion. We bought it, but we don't own it. We dedicated it for Kingdom use. We understand who we are in Christ, so we bring everything under the dominion of Christ. That is our mindset and we don't move from there no matter what the devil says.

The mistake Job made was to shift from his place of protection by having a mindset of fear. Fear removes you from the dominion of Christ and gives the devil access. Watch what Job chapter 3, verse 25 says:

Job 3:25
For the thing which I greatly feared is come upon me [emphasis added], **and that which I was afraid of is come unto me.**

When Job allowed fear to dominate his mind, he broke the hedge of protection and gave the devil access.

Know that you are in the ultimate place of protection—in Christ—and don't allow the lies of the devil to move you from there. Remember, the mind is where the enemy wages warfare, so that is where you must deal with him. Not by fighting, but by resisting him. Reject the lies he tries to plant in your mind and declare the truth about what the Word of God says about you.

Place everything you have under submission to the Word of God. When you start that business, don't go into it thinking "I own this business." Instead, go in with the awareness that you are in Christ, and bring that business into the place where you are. Bring it under the Lordship of Jesus. Declare He is the owner, and you are the manager of it.

The Bible tells us in Colossians 3:3 that your life is hidden.

Colossians 3:3
For ye are dead, and your life is hid with Christ in God.

Hallelujah! Job had a hedge of protection, but you've got something even better. You've got a divine cloaking shield. Not only can the devil not break through and touch you or anything you've got, he can't even see you. You've got supernatural stealth technology; it's called the Word of God. And the devil can't fight what he can't see. Just keep speaking the Word, and that's all he'll be able to detect.

You don't need to fight the devil in spiritual warfare. You only need to recognise who and where you are *in* Christ. Refuse to own anything. Place everything under the lordship of His Word and let go of the nuts!

Chapter Eight

The Intel of Warfare

Ramarni Wilfred of Loom Grove, Romford in the London region of England, has a recorded IQ higher than Bill Gates, Stephen Hawking and Albert Einstein. At just sixteen years old, he is already a five-year veteran of the Mensa Society. At eighteen months he was discussing the news and had already exhausted his favourite book, the Encyclopaedia Britannica. At two-years-old, he was bantering politics on his way to nursery school.

He is unquestionably one of the most brilliant minds of our time whose potential yet remains to be seen. His raw intellect seems surpassed only by his humility, refusing to compare himself with the likes of Einstein and Hawking, who he describes as true geniuses. He sums up the hullabaloo over his superior intellect with this insightful statement, "Having a high IQ isn't that important unless you do something really special with it."

You also have a high IQ, maybe not naturally but definitely spiritually. And it is your spiritual Intelligence Quotient (IQ) that separates those who need to fight the devil in spiritual warfare and those who don't. Spiritually, we are all born with the same IQ because we have the mind of Christ. The question is, what have you done with His mind? Intelligence Quotient is somewhat of a misnomer since nothing really gets divided. In actuality, IQ is an indication of how well one performs on mental tests which makes it a perfect frame of reference for spiritual warfare.

I want you to understand that intelligence is not the absence of ignorance. When young Ramarni was asked what it takes for him to be so clever, his response was, "It's probably a place of me not knowing something, and from that ignorance is like a desire to actually understand it, to know it." So, there is a level of ignorance that should spur you to activate, cultivate, and utilise the intelligence that you already have.

There is a level of intelligence that you need to have about the devil. Because as powerless as he is, there is a way that he can get an advantage in spiritual warfare. You have the mind of Christ, but if you do not use that mind intelligently to overcome ignorance, the devil will take advantage. The Bible says it this way in 2 Corinthians chapter 2, verse 11:

2 Corinthians 2:11
Lest Satan should get an advantage of us: for we are not ignorant of his devices.

That verse is telling us three things that we need to know to be most effective in spiritual warfare. We need to know that it is possible for a defeated foe, namely the devil, to gain an advantage over us. That in itself is a remarkable revelation. How could such a thing be possible? Well, the verse tells us that too. It says a certain kind of ignorance gives Satan an advantage. That begs the question, what kind of ignorance makes this possible?

Notice the keyword in that verse is the word "get." It doesn't say Satan "has" an advantage over us. We are the ones who have the advantaged position. But through ignorance of his devices, we can allow him to *get* an advantage. That means he doesn't have it unless you give it to him.

Now, the word "advantage" there is interesting. It is translated from the Greek word *pleonekteó*, which means to *overreach*. That lets us know there is a way that a Christian can allow the devil to reach too far.

I will keep reminding you that the devil is unarmed. He has no power, only tricks. He lures the naive Christian into fighting him in spiritual warfare by tricking them into believing lies. The devil was stripped of any ability to harm you. The only thing he's left with is his mouth. He talks. And when he speaks, the Bible says, he speaks his native tongue which is lies. In John chapter 8, Jesus told us that the devil is a liar and the father of lies.

John 8:44
Ye are of your father the devil, and the lusts of your father ye will do. He was a murderer from the beginning, and abode not in the truth, because there is no truth in him. When he speaketh a lie, he speaketh of his own: for he is a liar, and the father of it.

Everything the devil does goes back to one simple truth: he is a liar. That is crucial information because it helps us to understand how he operates.

Now, I want you to see something else in 2 Corinthians 2:11. Let's look at it again.

2 Corinthians 2:11
Lest Satan should get an advantage of us: for we are not ignorant of his devices.

Notice it says *devices*, which means he has more than one. He is defeated, so he resorts to devices. He uses many to lure you into a fight with him, different devices for different "attacks." But it's not the way you think.

When most Christians hear the word "devices," their minds immediately go to the physical, but there is nothing physical about these devices. The word "devices" comes from the Greek word *nóēma,* which is from the root word *noûs*, meaning *mind* or *understanding*. So, *nóēma* means a *thought*. The intelligent mind asks the question, how does a powerless devil attack? And since he is disarmed, what does he use to attack? The answer is simple. He uses devices, *thoughts*, and with those thoughts, he bombards the mind.

Every decision you make is a choice between minds, the mind of Christ and the carnal mind. The Bible tells us that the carnal mind is enmity against God. You'll find that in Romans chapter 8, verse 7:

Romans 8:7
Because the carnal mind is enmity against God: for it is not subject to the law of God, neither indeed can be.

It's only the carnal mind that is at war and fights with the devil. It is the carnal mind that is ignorant.

When we are told in 2 Corinthians 2:11 that we should not be ignorant of the Satan's devices, the word for "ignorant" is the Greek word *agnoéō*, which means *not to know through lack of information or intelligence*. The kind of intelligence to which this verse is referring is like what you would receive in times of warfare. It's a military term.

Military intelligence is information about an enemy that helps you to make winning strategic decisions. The purpose of gathering intelligence is to learn about your enemy's strengths and weaknesses. When it comes to the devil, his strength is his weakness, and his weakness is his strength. He is a liar. If you fail to understand that, when the devil uses his devices—his thoughts—to attack your mind with lies, that is one way he can get an advantage. But there is another way that is nearly as effective.

Knowing the devices your enemy uses in warfare is good, but it's not enough. You need more intelligence about how and when those devices will be used. The Bible tells us that we have a persistent adversary. He's been around longer than you, and he is an experienced adversary. He's not the least bit inventive—he uses the same old tricks he's been using. But he has used them for so long, he has developed a certain strategy for his attacks.

The Bible says something in the book of Ephesians that gives us intel on how the devil operates. Let's look at Ephesians chapter 6, and verse 11:

Ephesians 6:11
Put on the whole armour of God, that ye may be able to stand against the wiles of the devil.

There is a particular word there that I want you to pay close attention to, and that is the word *wiles*. The devil uses devices to attack the mind, but he uses wiles to determine when to carry out the attack. We saw in Chapter 2 that when the Bible speaks of the *wiles* of the devil, it is the word *methodeía*, which means *tricks* or *trickery*. It also means to *lie in wait*.

You see, the devil fights like the coward he is. Remember, he is full of fear. So, one of his tricks is to use the element of surprise. He is famous for ambush attacks. In warfare, when you want to carry out an ambush, you hide yourself and wait for just the right moment to launch your attack. That is precisely what he did when he tempted Jesus in the wilderness.

The Bible lets us know that Jesus was led into the wilderness to be tempted by the devil. And it says he fasted for forty days and forty nights. Let's pick it up from right there in Matthew chapter 4, verses 2 and 3:

Matthew 4:2-3
And when he had fasted forty days and forty nights, he was afterward an hungred. And when the tempter came to him, he said, If thou be the Son of God, command that these stones be made bread.

I want you to notice something. Jesus had completed His fast, "He *had fasted* forty days and forty nights." Then it says, "*afterward*" He was hungered. Now, notice when the devil came to Him and what he said.

...He was afterward an hungred. And when the tempter came to him, he said, If thou be the Son of God, command that these stones be made bread.

That was an ambush attack. The devil was lying in wait forty days and forty nights before he launched this particular attack.

Notice how strategic it was. As you can imagine, Jesus was very hungry, having not eaten for forty days and forty nights. And the devil comes with a well-planned lying thought, "*If* thou be the Son of God, command that these stones be made bread." Yes, the thought was designed to plant a seed of doubt, but the wiles can be seen *when* he tempted Jesus with the idea of bread. The enemy attacked in a way and at a time when he felt Jesus would be most vulnerable. Jesus was alone, isolated, hungry and physically weakened from hunger.

There is another detail that Christians often overlook about Jesus being in the wilderness, and that is given to us in Mark chapter 1 and verse 13:

Mark 1:13
And He was there in the wilderness forty days, tempted of Satan; and was with the wild beasts; and the angels ministered unto Him.

Jesus was surrounded by "wild beasts." And just in case you think the writer is just playing with words, "wild beasts" is translated from the Greek word *thēríon* which means *a dangerous animal, wild, venomous* and *ferocious*. When you are surrounded by ferocious and venomous animals, you don't sleep very well.

So, Jesus was physically exhausted. And don't for one moment think that the devil didn't try to trouble His mind until the forty days were ended. No! He was bombarding Jesus' mind with thoughts the whole time. So not only was Jesus physically exhausted, but He was also mentally exhausted.

All of those details give us intel not only about *how* the devil attacks—with devices, lying thoughts—but *when*. He lies in wait to ambush you when he thinks you are most vulnerable. That is why you'll notice that some of the worst attacks happen when you're not feeling well, or you're tired, alienated, isolated, alone, physically or mentally exhausted *and* after a great victory.

When Jesus was led by the Holy Ghost into the wilderness, He had just enjoyed one of the most exhilarating experiences He had while on Earth. It was the launch of His public ministry. Jesus was stepping into His purpose, fulfilling scripture and about to undertake the assignment for which He came to Earth. After being baptised by John, His cousin and forerunner, the crowning moment was the voice of His Father saying, "This is My beloved Son in whom I am well pleased."

Matthew 3:16-17
And Jesus, when he was baptised, went up straightway out of the water: and, lo, the heavens were opened unto him, and he saw the Spirit of God descending like a dove, and lighting upon him: And lo a voice from heaven, saying, This is my beloved Son, in whom I am well pleased.

On the heels of such a momentous occasion, that was when the devil attacked.

Now you have gathered some intelligence about how your enemy attacks and when. So, what should you do with it? The Bible tells us what to do in 1 Peter 5 and verse 8:

1 Peter 5:8
Be sober, be vigilant; because your adversary the devil, as a roaring lion, walketh about, seeking whom he may devour:

Now that you know that the devil has devices and is using wiles, lying in wait to try to ambush you, use that intelligence to be sober and vigilant.

Interestingly enough, both words mean *watch*, but they are not the same. The word "sober" is the Greek word *nēphō* which means to *watch* or be *sober*. The word "vigilant" comes from the Greek word *grēgoreúō*, which means *watch* or *watchful*. The first watch is a state of being, the second is a state of doing.

If you are walking, and I see that you are about to do something that could bring you or someone else harm, I could say, "Watch what you're doing!" It means I'm alerting you to the fact that you need to have your wits about you. Keep a clear head. Watch! That is a state of being. But if thieves have been spotted in the neighbourhood and I hire a security guard to stand outside my gate, I could tell him, "Be on your watch!" That is a state of doing. Do you see the difference?

Let me remind you, we are not speaking of physical things here. And that is where a lot of Christians get into trouble. I told you before that every decision you make is a choice between minds, the mind of Christ and the carnal mind. And the biggest problem with the carnal mind is that it's too intelligent but not in a way that maintains the advantage in spiritual warfare.

The carnal mind makes decisions based on what the world says, but it lacks the spiritual intelligence that is representative of the mind of Christ. It also lacks spiritual military intelligence about the devices of the devil. Both of these are the kind of intelligence which can only come by the Word of God.

You must make decisions with the mind of Christ. That means your decisions and your thought life in general are governed by the Word of God. You cannot be physically sober or vigilant and expect that is enough to keep the advantage when you're dealing with a spiritual enemy who's waiting to ambush you. The weapons of our warfare are not physical, but mighty *through God* to the pulling down of strongholds.

The mind of Christ is sober and vigilant. The mind that is governed by the Word of God is able to think clearly and override the lies the devil tries to plant. The mind of Christ is alert, fully aware that the devil is lurking about waiting for an opportunity to launch an ambush.

Being sober and being vigilant keeps you in the position of advantage in spiritual warfare. That's where you belong. You're not fighting with the devil, never! When you have the Word in you, you have enough spiritual intelligence to know that you don't need to fight the devil. And that prevents him from ever gaining any advantage over you in warfare.

Chapter Nine

Spiritual Thermal Conductivity

It was a balmy Thursday evening in Dallas, Texas, and the Kay Bailey Hutchison Convention Center was nearly filled to capacity. Seven thousand people had converged on the venue to attend the "Unleash the Power Within" conference hosted by motivational speaker, Tony Robbins. This was the first night of the conference, and the crowd was hanging on his every word hoping they would be the catalyst they needed to push them past their fears and limiting beliefs. While the participants were being fired up inside the arena, 12 to 15-foot beds of burning hot coals waited for them outside. It was time to "put your money where your mouth is" and take the firewalk challenge.

Participation in the firewalk is 100 per cent voluntary. But walking across the hot coals was the ultimate homage to their mentor and their own commitment to taking life by the horns. So, with the legalities of the required waiver behind them and the charismatic words of their life coach pushing them forward, most of the attendees took the walk to gain the coveted title "Firewalker."

Participants were encouraged to yell and scream to psyche themselves up as they tread across the coals. But that night, more than thirty of them were screaming in pain. Fear, distractions, and plain old doubt got the best of them, and their firewalk became a walk of shame. So ends the story of many people who fight the devil in spiritual warfare. The most famous of which is the account of the sons of Sceva.

The sons of Sceva were no strangers to the demonstrated power of God. They were familiar with Apostle Paul, through whom God wrought extraordinary miracles. According to the book of Acts, the sick were healed and evil spirits checked out just by coming in contact with a piece of cloth that had touched his body. Look at what it says in Acts chapter 19, verses 11 and 12:

Acts 19:11-12 AMPC
And God did unusual and extraordinary miracles by the hands of Paul. So that handkerchiefs or towels or aprons which had touched his skin were carried away and put upon the sick, and their diseases left them and the evil spirits came out of them.

Now, I want you to notice something in the next verse.

Acts 19:13
Then certain of the vagabond Jews, exorcists, took upon them to call over them which had evil spirits the name of the Lord Jesus, saying, We adjure you by Jesus whom Paul preacheth.

The Bible says *"then,"* after seeing the things Paul was doing. There were certain Jews who would wander around casting out evil spirits, but they were only using second-hand authority. They were simply copying what they saw Paul doing. These people didn't have a relationship with Jesus, so when they would try to cast out devils, they would command them out "by Jesus whom Paul preaches."

The seven sons of Sceva (a Jewish chief priest) decided they would try that too. So, they got together and started their own deliverance ministry. Contrary to what most people think, their ministry was extremely effective. Let's continue reading, and I'll show you why.

Acts 19:14-16
And there were seven sons of one Sceva, a Jew, and chief of the priests, which did so. And the evil spirit answered and said, Jesus I know, and Paul I know; but who are ye?

And the man in whom the evil spirit was leaped on them, and overcame them, and prevailed against them, so that they fled out of that house naked and wounded.

These guys, like some deliverance preachers today, thought the power to deal with devils was like a magic formula. They supposed they could use the name of Jesus like a password, that when the evil spirit heard it, he would just check out. But they got a rude awakening that day.

The Bible says the evil spirit was looking for something in the seven sons of Sceva that he did not find. This evil spirit ran a quick check on all seven of the brothers and didn't find the one thing that would force him out. So, for his trouble, using the body he possessed, he forced them out instead. The Bible says he overcame all seven of them, beat them silly, tore the clothes off them, and chased them out into the street.

The seven sons of Sceva were so effective that the evil spirit they were trying to cast out became a deliverance preacher. When the people saw what the evil spirit did to the sons of Sceva, that by itself preached a powerful message about the name of Jesus. Watch what it says in verses 17 through 20:

Acts 19:17-20
And this was known to all the Jews and Greeks also dwelling at Ephesus; and fear fell on them all, and the name of the Lord Jesus was magnified. And many that believed came, and confessed, and shewed their deeds. Many of them also which used curious arts brought their books together, and burned them before all men: and they counted the price of them, and found it fifty thousand pieces of silver. So mightily grew the word of God and prevailed.

The evil spirit understood one thing that the sons of Sceva did not. Let me explain.

In Matthew 28:18, Jesus declared, "all power is given unto Me in heaven and in earth." Without looking at the original language, you will never understand what Jesus was saying. You see, there are two Greek words translated 'power' in the New Testament, *dunamis* and *exousía*. Acts chapter 1, verse 8 says:

Acts 1:8a
But ye shall receive power, after that the Holy Ghost is come upon you...

The word translated "power" in that verse is *dunamis*, which refers to *inherent power*. This is power that comes from the Holy Ghost. It is the *dynamic ability to cause changes*. But when

Jesus said, "all power is given unto Me," He was not talking about *dunamis*. He was referring to *exousía*.

Jesus said, "all *exousía* is given unto Me." That kind of power to which He was referring is *delegated authority* or *the right to act for another*. Now, I want you to follow me carefully here because this is where a lot of Christians miss it and why they have sons of Sceva kinds of experiences with demons.

A lot of Christians read that verse, and when they find themselves dealing with devils, they think Jesus is the one with the power. So, they use Jesus' name like they expect Him to come and do what needs to be done. Then they are surprised when they don't get the results they expected. Now, I'm about to tell you something that will shock you. *Jesus doesn't have the power.* And it's when you're ignorant of that divine fact that you'll find yourself struggling with devils.

Now, watch what the Bible says in Luke chapter 10 and verse 19:

Luke 10:19
Behold...

Stop right there. That word means *awaken to the reality* of what I'm about to tell you. With that in mind, let's continue.

Luke 10:19
Behold, I give unto you power to tread on serpents and scorpions, and over all the power of the enemy: and nothing shall by any means hurt you.

Reading that verse in the English will lead you to believe that the two instances of the word 'power' are the same, but they are not. It really reads like this:

Behold, I give unto you *exousía* to tread on serpents and scorpions, and over all the *dunamis* of the enemy: and nothing shall by any means hurt you.

Before I go any further, let me remind you once again that the devil doesn't have any power unless he gets it from you. If he can get you to believe and act on his lies, then he'll use *your* power against you, just like he did with Adam. But he has no power of his own. What he has is an inherent ability to lie. But you have something greater; you have authority.

Authority is why a 44-kg traffic warden can stop a 44-ton semi-trailer truck. The warden doesn't have to have muscles or be a giant, but he has the power to stop your vehicle no matter what size it is. All he has to do is hold one hand up—not even two—and you'll have to stop in your tracks. Even if he's sick that day and he's coughing while telling you to stop, you'll have to stop. Maybe he's not paying his rent while he's stopping you, or perhaps his marriage is falling apart. None of that matters because he has authority, and when he says stop, everything pays attention.

That's the kind of authority that you have, the sort of power that you possess. When you tell the devil "stop in your tracks right there, you are not going any further," those demons have no choice but to pay attention to what you have said. Why? Because you have the authority; you were given power of attorney. The same authority Jesus used when He said all exousía is given to Me, you have it!

Understand the power that we're talking about here. You're not functioning for Him; you're functioning as Him. It's not by your might, it's by the Jesus in you that you are able to stop the devil in his tracks. That is why the sons of Sceva were beaten by the devil. They called the name of Jesus without the revelation of who He is. They were trying to use second-hand authority, and it doesn't work like that. When that evil spirit looked for Jesus in them, he couldn't find Him. But that is not the case with you. Christ is in you, and you have the authority to put the devil and his cohorts in check, and that authority is absolute. No demon can resist it.

This authority you have over the devil has nothing to do with mind over matter. You can't psyche yourself up for this one. Let's look at the verse again, and I'll show you what I mean. Luke 10:19 says:

Luke 10:19
Behold, I give unto you exousía to tread on serpents and scorpions, and over all the dunamis of the enemy: and nothing shall by any means hurt you.

Now, the word "tread" is rendered from the Greek word *patéō*. It means to walk in a specified way. You can't just tread on serpents and scorpions any way you feel like. There is a specific way to do it using spiritual thermal conductivity. For you to understand spiritual thermal conductivity, I will first explain how thermal conductivity works and then show you the spiritual application of it.

The reason some of the attendees of the "Unleash the Power Within" conference got their feet burned is that they didn't walk in a specified way. They didn't understand the principle of thermal conductivity. Now watch this, because I'm about to take the mystery out of walking on hot coals and how to tread on serpents and scorpions.

Thermal conductivity is an object's ability to transfer energy in the form of heat to another object. Coal is mostly carbon, which is terrible when it comes to conducting heat. A hot coal is also covered with a layer of ash, which is an even less effective conductor. So, you have something that is already bad at transferring heat (coal) encased in something even worse at conducting heat (ash). So, because the hot coal doesn't have power when it comes to the transfer of heat energy, you can walk on them, but you have to walk in the specified way.

If you spend time lingering over each coal instead of briskly walking across them, there's a risk of being burned. And if you run across the coals, your feet will sink deeper into the layer of ash which will also increase your chances of being burned. Now, there's one more piece of information you need in order to understand how thermal conductivity applies to spiritual warfare.

If you fill a paper cup with water and place it over a flame, the cup will not catch on fire. You see, paper ignites at a temperature of 232 degrees Celsius (450 degrees Fahrenheit). And water changes from a liquid to a gas (steam) at 100 degrees Celsius (212 degrees Fahrenheit). Since the water is in constant contact with the cup, the paper cup can't get any hotter than 100 degrees Celsius, which is well below the temperature necessary for it to catch on fire. In other words, the water inside the cup protects it from any danger of burning up.

What does that have to do with walking on hot coals or spiritual warfare? There was something the conference attendees and those fighting devils in spiritual warfare missed. The blood flowing through your body keeps you from getting burned by the hot coals in the same way water prevents the cup from lighting on fire. In other words, there is something in you that protects you from getting harmed in that way. Now, here is where your mind comes into the equation.

When you're in a heightened state of fear, your body's blood vessels constrict so there's less blood flowing through your feet and therefore less protection from being burned by the hot coals. But, if you maintain the right state of mind and you are aware of what is inside you, your blood will flow freely and protect your feet.

Treading on serpents and scorpions sounds dangerous, but it's not. Spiritually, there is also a state of mind that you must maintain. You must know that you have spiritual thermal conductivity. There is Someone inside of you, and His presence should cause you to walk in the specified way understanding that no harm can come to you. Otherwise, the devil will lie to you and try to get you to believe that he can "burn" you, but he can't. He's nothing but ash, a remnant of what he used to be. He is as cold as the snake he is. He has no fire in him. You are the one carrying the fire because Christ is in you. So, when you walk in your authority and tread on the devil, you can't linger or run in fear because fear short circuits the power of God. You must walk confidently in your authority, understanding that the One who already defeated the devil is inside you.

There is no ability the devil has that can do anything to you. The Bible says, "*nothing* shall by *any means* harm you." You can tread on him with no fear. Jesus said I gave you authority, exousía, to tread, *patéō* on serpents and scorpions. Patéō also means to *crush with your feet* and *treat with insult or contempt*. That's also part of walking in the specified way. Not only are you crushing the enemy, but you are also insulting him. You are treating him with contempt, and there's nothing he can do about it. *Nothing* shall by any means hurt you. Notice it does not say some things will not hurt you or a quarter of the things in life will hurt you? It says nothing, zilch, zero! Nothing at all shall hurt you.

Not only do you possess absolute power, but you are also in the place of absolute protection. Many Christians are familiar with Psalm 91. It is a common go-to passage of scripture that talks about protection. It begins like this:

Psalm 91:1
He that dwelleth in the secret place of the most High shall abide under the shadow of the Almighty.

Preachers all over the world will tell you that the "secret place" is a place of protection. They are right, but most preachers misinterpret what the secret place is. It is true that if you dwell in the secret place of the Most High, you are under the protection of the Almighty. The question is, where is the secret place of the Most High? And the answer is, He is the Secret Place. It tells you right there in the next verse, but many Christians miss it. Let's read verses 1 and 2 together:

Psalm 91:1-2
He that dwelleth in the secret place of the most High shall abide under the shadow of the Almighty. I will say *of the Lord,* **He is my refuge and my fortress: my God; in** *him* **will I trust [emphasis added].**

Dwelling in the Secret Place of the Most High means dwelling in God. Paul puts it this way, "**if any man be in Christ, he is a new creature**" (2 Corinthians 5:17). Christ is that Secret Place, that dwelling place. You are *in* Him, and He is your refuge and fortress. That means you have spiritual thermal conductivity inside and out. Christ is in you, protecting you from the inside out, and you are in Christ, protecting you from the outside in. You are protected from every possible angle, so you can exercise your authority without fear.

You have the right to command things into action. You have the right to speak, and things will listen to you. The moment you say something, it has to happen. Why? Because you were given the power, the authority to tread upon serpents. If poverty is the serpent in your life, then you have the power to tread upon poverty. If sickness is the scorpion, then you have the authority to tread upon that sickness, and it will have no choice but to check out of your body. You have the authority. It doesn't say this power is only for pastors, apostles or prophets. You have the power!

Once you know the truth, that you were given the power, all you need to do is speak the Word, and it's done. You have jurisdiction over sickness. You have jurisdiction in your family. You can speak your whole family back together again. If anything is broken, you can speak it to life. Your authority is greater than any power the devil has because the only power he has is tricks designed to get you to believe his lies.

Chapter Ten

When Paul Fought the Devil

A few years ago, I stood in an open-air service in Harare with thousands in attendance, and I began to minister the Gospel. The Lord had given me a word for the people that had gathered that day, and it was like fire shut up in my bones. I could sense the anointing, and I knew destinies were going to change that day. Not long into my sermon, it started to rain, I mean heavy equatorial rainfall. I could tell the crowd was now a little bit distracted by the rain, but they were not moved because I did not stop preaching.

Now, as a prophet of God, I have stopped the rain before, simply by exercising my authority in the name of Jesus. I thought to myself, this is one occasion that I needed to do this because I knew what the Lord had instructed me for that day, and I was not going to let the rain stop me. Right in the middle of my sermon, I lifted up my voice and commanded the rain to stop in the name of Jesus. Much to the delight of the crowd, immediately the rain fizzled out, and I continued to minister.

Twenty minutes later it started to rain again. At this point in time, I was beginning to get frustrated. I didn't understand how the rain I had just commanded to stop in the name of Jesus could return a few minutes later. I did that three more times, and each time, after twenty minutes, it would come back.

You see, everything I say and do has to be according to the Word of God. And I knew and understood from scripture that we have the authority over the elements in the name of Jesus. That means when the rain hears my command in the name Jesus, it is as if it has heard the voice of Jesus himself and should respond accordingly. And yes, you read that one correctly, the rain hears, but that's another subject for another time.

So, I asked the Lord if there was anything I was missing. After all, I had done this before, and it had worked every time. He said to me, "Son, I am not only your Father, I am your Lord, and when I sent you to preach today, I knew it was going to rain. You are a soldier, and whether it rains or the sun shines, My mission on earth will be fulfilled. My grace is sufficient for you, and for that reason only, I have allowed the rain to continue. Keep preaching for soldiers can withstand any weather. 'Preach the word; be instant in season and out of season...' Remember when I said that in 2 Timothy 4, verse 2? My Grace is sufficient for you."

When I heard those words, I felt like Jackie Chan on steroids! I carried on preaching in that rain, and many were touched by the Spirit of God. We witnessed many miracles that day, more than we had ever done before that time. So, what was the Lord trying to teach me that day? He said my grace is sufficient for you. Immediately I was reminded of the example of the apostle Paul that many like to use in error to demonstrate just how powerful the devil is. Watch what the scripture says:

2 Corinthians 12:7-8
And lest I should be exalted above measure through the abundance of the revelations, there was given to me a thorn

in the flesh, the messenger of Satan to buffet me, lest I should be exalted above measure. For this thing I besought the Lord thrice, that it might depart from me.

Now, Paul tells us here that he had a thorn in the flesh, and many mistakenly quickly make the assumption that this thorn in the flesh was an illness that Paul was suffering from. You cannot be further from the truth.

Where did you ever read in the Bible that Paul's thorn in the flesh was an illness? It's simply not scriptural. Study the Scriptures. See how the Bible uses that term. In the Old Testament, God said to Israel, "If you don't kill those Canaanites when you possess the land, they will be thorns in your side. They will torment you."

Numbers 33:55
But if ye will not drive out the inhabitants of the land from before you; then it shall come to pass, that those which ye let remain of them shall be pricks in your eyes, and thorns in your sides, and shall vex you in the land wherein ye dwell.

In that passage, God was merely telling the children of Israel that unless they completely destroy the enemy, he would recuperate and fight them again. He was not talking of some disease that would come upon them. He said the Canaanites would be a thorn in their flesh. Now that Apostle Paul takes the exact expression and uses it, theologians are already talking about some disease.

Joshua 23:13
Know for a certainty that the Lord your God will no more drive out any of these nations from before you; but they shall be

snares and traps unto you, and scourges in your sides, and thorns in your eyes, until ye perish from off this good land which the Lord your God hath given you.

Consistently in scripture, you will find the expression "thorn in the flesh" was never used to talk about a plague or any form of sickness, but the Lord used it to refer to the activities of the enemy. In fact, Paul himself tells us exactly what the thorn was: "the messenger of Satan to buffet me." Everywhere Paul went to preach, this evil spirit that he called the messenger of Satan went before and behind him and stirred up everything it could.

Paul couldn't command the evil spirit to leave the earth because the devil has the right to be here until Adam's lease runs out. Paul felt helpless to evict this demonic entity and banish it completely from the planet earth. It was not because this demon was so powerful, but because until Adam's lease on the earth runs out, that demon has the right to stay on the earth and go wherever it wants. That is why when the Lord Jesus was being tempted of the devil, the Bible says the devil departed until an opportune time. That means he came back again. He still had the right to go wherever he pleased.

You need to understand that Paul had no issues casting out devils. He even taught on the subject. In fact, in his letter to the Ephesians, he was telling them how we are seated far above principalities and powers, the demonic ranks.

Ephesians 2:6
And hath raised *us* up together, and made *us* sit together in heavenly *places* in Christ Jesus [emphasis added].

Just like me when I faced the unrelenting rain, he knew how to deal with the demonic, but I don't what you to miss the Lord's response to Paul's prayer.

2 Corinthians 12:8-9 NKJV
Concerning this thing I pleaded with the Lord three times that it might depart from me. And He said to me, "My grace is sufficient for you, for My strength is made perfect in weakness." Therefore most gladly I will rather boast in my infirmities, that the power of Christ may rest upon me.

The Lord said, "My grace is sufficient for you." In other words, He was saying, *Paul, this thing that you are bringing before Me, I have already given you the ability to overcome. Don't you realise Paul, you already have what it takes to be victorious. My victory is yours. There is no need to even pray about the devil. My grace is sufficient for you*!

Paul never prayed that same prayer again. He knew how to grow in grace, and the Lord had just told him, as for this situation, My grace is all you need. Brothers and sisters, you can choose to grow in grace and keep the enemy at bay. I said it's a choice because you can actually decide to do something about it. Watch what the scripture says:

2 Peter 3:18
But grow in grace, and in the knowledge of our Lord and Saviour Jesus Christ. To him be glory both now and for ever. Amen.

You can grow in grace through your knowledge of the Word of God.

The scripture says, grow in grace the knowledge of our Lord Jesus Christ. That means the more Word you have, the more grace you have. The level of grace you operate with right now is directly proportional to how much of God's Word you actually know. Knowledge of God's Word will impart His grace to you.

That means there is no fixed measure to the grace that you can have. It is only determined by your level of knowledge.

Romans 5:17
For if by one man's offence death reigned by one; much more they which receive abundance of grace and of the gift of righteousness shall reign in life by one, Jesus Christ.

The Bible says, *"they which receive abundance of grace."* That means grace can be measured. People are receiving it in different measures according to their knowledge of God's Word. So, he says the ones that can get an abundance of grace shall reign in this life as kings. They will be masters over their own destinies, over the elements and Satan cannot lord it over them. When the Word of God dwells in you richly, you have just set yourself up for the abundance of grace. Hallelujah!

Chapter Eleven

Spiritual Kwashiorkor

It is estimated that one billion people around the world suffer from inadequate protein intake. The most severe form of protein deficiency is called kwashiorkor. According to the leading health organizations in the world, kwashiorkor is found mainly in underdeveloped and developing countries. That is what the statistics say, but they are mistaken. Kwashiorkor is found mostly in the Church.

The reason so many Christians find themselves fighting the devil is because they are suffering from spiritual kwashiorkor. Their spiritual diet is lacking in the meat of the Word. Just as with physical kwashiorkor, when untreated, spiritual kwashiorkor leads to the loss of muscle mass, lowering of the immune system, and mental disabilities. In other words, you become spiritually weak, vulnerable and mentally disturbed, all detrimental if you are embroiled in spiritual warfare.

The Bible tells us that the devil goes around like a roaring lion looking for someone to devour.

1 Peter 5:8
Be sober, be vigilant; because your adversary the devil, as a roaring lion, walketh about, seeking whom he may devour

Notice it says whom he *may* devour. If he's looking for people whom he *may* devour, that implies that there are people whom he may not devour. That means there are some Christians who are susceptible to falling prey to the tricks of the devil and some who are not. What makes the difference between the two is one has spiritual kwashiorkor, and the other does not.

The Bible says the devil goes about like a roaring lion. Now, I want you to understand that a lion has a certain way of attacking its prey, particularly large prey like an elephant, for example. Pound for pound, a lion is no match for an elephant. The adult male African elephant, the largest land animal in the world, weighs in at an average of nearly 6,000 kilograms (13,000 pounds). But an adult male lion averages only about 190 kilograms (420 pounds), a minuscule 3 per cent of the massive elephant's size. However, the greatest advantage an adult elephant has over an adult lion is not its size, but it's age.

You see, lions have distinct roars, and each one has its own meaning. The Bible tells us that there is no voice or sound without meaning. 1 Corinthians 14:10 says:

1 Corinthians 14:10
There are, it may be, so many kinds of voices in the world, and none of them is without signification.

The word translated there as "voices" is rendered from the Greek word *phōné* which means *noise*, *voice*, or *sound*. So, the lion roars, but only the mature elephant can discern its subtle cues, which gives the elephant the greatest advantage even long before the lion gets anywhere close. The mature elephant knows how to position itself when it hears the roar. The immature elephant, on the other hand, is no match for the experienced flesh-eating predator.

An adult lion poses the greatest threat to the young and the weak. That is what makes spiritual kwashiorkor so dangerous and potentially fatal. The immature Christian lacks the spiritual weight, active defence system, and mental clarity that only the knowledge of the Word can bring. When the devil is seeking whom he may devour, he looks for those in the Church who are suffering from spiritual kwashiorkor. That is why deliverance is needed.

My son, Prophet Shepherd Bushiri, has deliverance services often, and demons are cast out regularly. I cast out devils. But have you ever wondered why with all the casting out of devils that we do, we ourselves don't need to be delivered? Why is it that the pastor is delivering you and you are not delivering him? Why are demons coming out of you but not him? The answer is simple. The reason why I am not running around screaming because of demons in me is that there is no demon in me. That proves I am more mature than the people I deliver. Is there a need for deliverance? Emphatically, yes! But it is my duty as a minister to deal with spiritual kwashiorkor and get the spiritually immature to my level so I will not have to continue delivering them.

As we read in previous chapters, all the devil has is *wiles*, *methodeía* in the Greek, which means *tricks*. That means you need a sure-fire way to win against these tricks. The Bible tells us that to deal with the tricks of the enemy, we must be aware of his devices, and we must also be able to stand.

In 2 Corinthians chapter 2, verse 11, Paul says this:

2 Corinthians 2:11
Lest Satan should get an advantage of us: for we are not *ignorant of his devices* [emphasis added].

So, what defeats immature Christians is that they are ignorant of the devil's devices. That's one thing that gives Satan an advantage. But the other thing that gives him an advantage is the immature Christian is unable to stand. Paul says we must do everything to stand, and then stand.

Ephesians 6:13-14a
Wherefore take unto you the whole armour of God, that ye may be able to withstand in the evil day, and having done all, to stand. Stand therefore...

You see, the Bible says, "Stand therefore." That is not telling you to stand up in the flesh. It's telling you to stand up in the spirit. But if you have spiritual kwashiorkor, your legs are too weak to stand. That's when you will be defeated by the devil and possessed, and that's why you will need deliverance.

Force Your Spiritual Diet on Yourself

When a child is young, he can eat and eat and eat. But some children don't want to eat. All they want to do is to play, play, play. Even if you cook the best meal, they want to play. They can be hungry, they may even say "I want something to eat," but they want to play more than they want to eat. They can open their mouth and put food in there, but before they have a chance to finish chewing it properly, they run back to play.

That is what happens in the spirit. We have issues of people who are not mature in the Lord but are not aware that what they need is the food of the Spirit, the Word of God. Because they don't eat spiritual food, these spiritual babies lack protein (the meat of the Word), which leads to spiritual kwashiorkor. As a result, they will not be able even to move much less stand up.

The good news is spiritual kwashiorkor can be reversed and completely eradicated with the proper diet. You won't need deliverance if you just eat properly. People come to me because they want me to deliver them from eye problems. *Man of God deliver me. I can't see! The devil is attacking my eyes!* Yet I tell people over and over, you wouldn't need deliverance if you would just drink water. When you don't drink enough water, the body becomes dehydrated and starts to draw water from wherever it can. It starts with the weakest parts of the body, which are the eyes. That's why I tell you if you changed your diet you wouldn't need deliverance.

The word of God is what builds you up. Look at what the Bible says in Acts chapter 20, verse 32:

Acts 20: 32
And now, brethren, I commend you to God, and to the word of his grace, which is able to build you up, and to give you an inheritance among all them which are sanctified.

The spirit feeds on the Word the same way the physical body feeds on food. You have to consume the Word. But you need to understand that just as with physical kwashiorkor, if a child has gone without sufficient protein for a long time, eating again can be a shock to their system. Therefore, food must be introduced or reintroduced carefully. That is why ministers of the Word need to be mature so that they don't try to feed a ribeye to someone who is only ready for a burger.

I recently decided to go vegetarian. But before you go cutting meat out of your diet, let me explain my version of vegetarian. I only eat vegetables and things that eat vegetables. That means if a cow eats vegetables, I can eat cow. (And in case you didn't know, grass is considered a vegetable.)

Now, there are people who were vegetarians for decades—no meat—then they decided to start eating meat again. They can't just run out and try to eat a 72-ounce Texas steak as if they were trying to catch up for all the meat they've missed over the years. No! Experts will tell you that you have to gradually introduce protein into the diet to prevent complications. The key is quality and consistency. You are eating, consuming the Word, every day. You have a part to play in this, and ministers also have a part.

Your duty is to be in the Word every day. Start with the Good News Daily, which is bite-sized quality meat that you can chew on every day. You don't have to get up and think about what you should read that day. It's laid out for you right there. Then be where the Word is.

I'm always amazed at people, women in particular, who say they want to be married, but as soon as service is over, they make a beeline for the door. There are single men all over the church. But these women rush out as if they think angel Gabriel is going to show up at their door with a man, gift-wrapped with a gift bow on his head. *I have come from the presence of the Lord to tell you that this is your husband.* No, it doesn't work like that! Be where the thing you want is.

The same is true of the Word, and this goes beyond just wanting; this is a dire need. You *must* have it. So, you must be where the Word is. We are privileged to be living in a time where the Word is available in abundance, a virtual cornucopia of the Word. We have it available in different mediums. You can pick up your physical Bible, or you can pull it up on your phone. You can go to church freely and hear the Word being ministered. You can tune into Good News TV on channel Sky 596, or tune into the live streams when the Word is taught on our social media platforms. There is no excuse for you to be spiritually malnourished. The Word is available in abundance!

If ministers don't minister the Word, they will be forced to minister deliverance. They will need continual deliverance from having to minister deliverance continually. In Luke chapter 6, Jesus said the blind cannot lead the blind; otherwise, both of them will end up in the same situation.

Luke 6:39
Can the blind lead the blind? shall they not both fall into the ditch?

You cannot take someone where you are not. You cannot lead someone where you haven't been. That means that every minister has a responsibility—an obligation—to know the Word for themselves.

Paul said something exciting in Colossians chapter 1 and verse 25. He says:

Colossians 1:25
Whereof I am made a minister, according to the dispensation of God which is given to me for you, to fulfil the word of God

Paul says, "I am made a *minister*… to fulfil the Word of God." Now, that word minister is what I want to draw your attention to. It is translated from the Greek word *diákonos* which means *a waiter*. If you look at that verse in the Amplified version, it reads this way:

Colossians 1:25 AMPC
In it *I became a minister* in accordance with the divine stewardship which was entrusted to me for you [as its object and for your benefit], *to make the Word of God fully known* [*among you*, emphasis added]

When you go to a restaurant, the waiter brings the food to where you are and serves it to you. That's what a minister does. A minister serves the Word to you.

Let's say you went to eat at a health food restaurant. The waiter, who also happens to be the one who prepared the food, comes out to serve you. The only problem is he looks weak and emaciated and can hardly stand. You would likely do one of two things, ask for another waiter or go to a different restaurant. The quality of the food may be exceptional, but as they say in the culinary world, presentation is everything. If you go to a place that is known for serving food that promotes good health, the servers should reflect that which they are serving. No one wants their food served to them by someone who looks like they are two feet away from death, sucking on a lifesaver.

You cannot help someone else to stand when your own legs are rickety and weak with spiritual kwashiorkor. You cannot deliver anybody until you have delivered yourself over to the Word. If you try it, you yourself will need deliverance. Engaging in spiritual warfare when you have spiritual kwashiorkor is like inviting the devil to dinner with you served on a plate. If left unremedied, the effects of kwashiorkor are you cannot stand, you are vulnerable to attack, and you are mentally disturbed. That affects all three areas that you need to be effective in spiritual warfare. You need to stand; you need to remain behind an impenetrable defence system, and you need your mind—the mind of Christ in you—to be fully functional. Spiritual kwashiorkor must be eradicated, and the only remedy is the Word.

Chapter Twelve

Resisting the Devil with Spiritual Inertia

On the afternoon of April 12th, 1912, a British passenger luxury liner called the Titanic set sail from Dock Gate 4, Berth 44 at the port in Southampton, England. It was the ship's maiden voyage. From bow to stern, the Titanic was a 52,000 ton, 882 foot-long marvel of engineering. It was powered by one turbine engine that drove the ship's main propeller and two reciprocating engines which powered the side propellers. The force of the vortex created by the engines was so powerful, it would pull in nearby ships. Producing a staggering 51,000 horsepower, the ship was nearly forty-two times faster than the Bugatti Veyron Super Sport, the fastest car in the world. The ship was equipped with sixteen watertight compartments designed to protect it from flooding. The Titanic was thought to be unstoppable and unsinkable.

But on the night of April 14th, around 11:40 PM, the starboard or right side of the Titanic struck a mass of ice in the North Atlantic, rupturing five watertight compartments below the waterline. Less than three hours later, the unstoppable, unsinkable Titanic was submerged beneath the waves.

What I'm about to share with you will cause you to put the devil on the run and have a lot of fun. It's vital that you get it. Otherwise, the devil will gain an advantage over you when it comes to spiritual warfare, and you'll sink faster than the Titanic.

In physics, there is something called the law of inertia, otherwise known as Newton's First Law of Motion. It is often stated as follows:

An object at rest will remain at rest, and an object in motion will remain in motion unless acted upon by some external net force.

Newton's First Law defines inertia, which in simple terms is the ability of an object to resist changes in motion. Let me show you how this works and how it applies to spiritual warfare.

Let me start by explaining that inertia is not a force. Inertia is what remains when you take all other forces away. You need to apply force to get an object moving. And if it is already moving, force must be applied to slow it down to a stop. If an object has more mass, it will require more force to move it than what an object with less mass would require.

For example, a sailboat can be moved into motion by a gust of wind. But a ship, like the Titanic, has a mass that is much greater than a sailboat. Therefore, it requires the force of 51,000 horsepower engines to cause it to move from a state of rest. A tremendous amount of force is required both to get it going and to stop it. The more massive the object, the more inertia it has. In other words, it is capable of resisting greater force.

Now, the devil comes to try to attack by force. The problem for him is he does not have the power to move anything, and he does not have enough mass to resist when faced with a greater force. And that force is the Greater One inside you. That's what the Bible tells us in 1 John chapter 4, verse 4:

1 John 4:4
Ye are of God, little children, and have overcome them: because greater is he that is in you, than he that is in the world.

Brothers and sisters, the Greater One is inside you! Do you understand what that means? You might ask, greater than what? He's greater than whatever you need Him to be greater than. And the Bible is letting you know in no uncertain terms that He is greater than the devil. In fact, Muhammad Ali was sorely mistaken when he said, "I am the greatest!" The truth is Jesus is the greatest! And He's inside you, hallelujah!

The devil can't do a thing with Jesus. He's too big for the devil and completely resistant to anything the devil tries to do. And you are in Him, which means the devil can't do anything to you either. When the devil tries to attack you, he is really attacking Christ, and that's like a ping pong ball hurling itself at Mount Kilimanjaro. The Bible says it this way in Matthew 21 and verse 44:

Matthew 21:44
And whosoever shall fall on this stone shall be broken: but on whomsoever it shall fall, it will grind him to powder.

That was Jesus speaking, and He was talking about Himself. He is that Rock that grinds anything that comes against Him to powder! The Greater One inside you gives you spiritual inertia, a supernatural ability to resist the devil's schemes. So, the devil can't force you to do anything. In fact, he is the one who can be forced. He has zero inertia. The Bible tells us this in Colossians 2, verse 15, where it says:

Colossians 2:15
And having spoiled principalities and powers, he made a shew of them openly, triumphing over them in it.

Jesus went down to Hell, and the devil and his cohorts tried to bum-rush Him. They grabbed Him and tried to take Him down by force. But the Bible tells us that Jesus simply *shook them off*. The Weymouth translation paints the picture for us.

Colossians 2:15 Weymouth
And the hostile princes and rulers *He shook off from Himself* [emphasis added], and boldly displayed them as His conquests, when by the Cross He triumphed over them.

The devil and his gang were no match for Jesus. They gave it their best shot, all the force they had, and they couldn't move Him, not even one millimetre. His mass in the realm of the Spirit was too great, and His spiritual inertia made Him immovable and unstoppable. And that immovable, unstoppable Jesus is inside you!

Now, I want you to see this. The Bible says that after Jesus' triumphant victory over the devil, He ascended far above all the heavens and took his position of rest. The Bible says it this way in Ephesians chapter 4, verses 9 and 10:

Ephesians 4:9-10
(Now that He ascended, what is it but that He also descended first into the lower parts of the earth? He that descended is the same also that ascended up far above all heavens, that he might fill all things.)

Let me just interject this point right here and shock you a little bit. Jesus is *not* in Heaven. Just let that marinate for a moment. Now, go back and read again the verses we just read. It says that Jesus ascended "far above *all heavens*." That means He is not in Heaven; He is in a place far above *all* heavens.

Not only did He ascend far above all the heavens, but He also took a position of rest. He is seated at the right hand of God. Watch what Mark chapter 16, verse 19 says:

Mark 16:19
So then after the Lord had spoken unto them, he was received up into heaven, and sat on the right hand of God.

You will find similar language in Hebrews chapter 10 and verse 12:

Hebrews 10:12
But this man [Jesus], after He had offered one sacrifice for sins for ever, sat down on the right hand of God

Jesus is seated at the right hand of God. Now, the "right hand" does not mean He is on the right side of God. Right hand refers to His position of authority. But the point I'm making here is that He is seated. That is a position of rest.

Remember, mass is a measurement of an object's inertia, and inertia is the ability of an object to resist change. The more mass an object has, the more inertia it has. We've already seen that the devil did not have the force required to move Jesus from His place of rest. But here's the thing: I told you before, the devil is a sore loser. So what he does now is to try to fight against you.

Fighting is the use of force designed to move you from a position of victory and rest to defeat. So, it's understandable that the devil would try to fight you because he recognizes, even if you don't, that you are already in a position of victory. Therefore, his goal is to try to move you from that position. He knows he cannot, but he bets on you not knowing that. So, when you fight the devil in spiritual warfare, it is a ridiculous notion, because you are fighting with a personality who has already been defeated.

The devil doesn't have the force required to move you from your position of rest. You were never supposed to fight the devil. You are supposed to activate the law of spiritual inertia, Christ in you, and remain at rest. James chapter 4, verse 7 tells us how to do this. He says:

James 4:7
Submit yourselves therefore to God. Resist the devil, and he will flee from you.

There is no fighting involved in that verse. There is no place that tells you to fight the devil. It says you are to *resist* him.

Now, the word "resist" is rendered from the Greek word *anthístēmi*, which means *resist* or *withstand*. This does not mean resisting in the sense of struggling against someone or something. No! Literally, it means to *stand against*. So, you are standing, not struggling. What makes this resistance so powerful is that it is not based on your action but your location. You see, there is a prerequisite to resisting the devil, and it is that prerequisite that makes resisting powerful.

Before you can resist the devil, there is something you must do. The first part of James 4, verse 7 tells us that we must *submit* ourselves to God. That explains why some Christians think they are resisting the devil only to find themselves being pushed around by him. On your own, you have no spiritual mass or inertia, but when you submit yourself to God, you become as immovable as He is.

The word translated "submit" is derived from the Greek word *hupotassó* which is a combination of two Greek words: *hupo*, which means *under* and *tassó*, which means *to arrange in an orderly fashion*. Using those two definitions, to submit means *to arrange in an orderly fashion under*. One of the interesting things about the word *hupotassó* is that it is a military term. It refers to the arranging of troops in a military fashion under the command of a leader in order to carry out effective warfare.

You cannot effectively resist the devil until you position yourself under the Word. And how do you do that? It's simple. Let the Word be the Commander of your life. Fall in line with the Word. The more Word you have in you, the more your spiritual mass and your ability to resist the devil increases.

1 John 1, verse 1 tells us exactly who the Word is, but most Christians don't realize to whom this verse is referring. It says:

1 John 1:1
In the beginning was the Word, and the Word was with God, and the Word was God.

Now, if you go over to Revelation chapter 19, verse 13, you will see that the Word is Jesus. It reads like this:

Revelation 19:13
And He [Jesus] was clothed with a vesture dipped in blood: and
His name is called The Word of God **[emphasis added].**

Did you see that? Jesus *is* the Word of God!

I want you to understand that it's not that Christ gets bigger in you as you submit to the Word. He's already as big as He's ever going to be, so He's not increasing. But the more Word you have in you, the more aware you become of how massive He is in you. You are awakening to the reality of His bigness in you. Then you can boldly say what He said in Matthew 21, verse 44:

Matthew 21:44
And whosoever shall fall on this stone shall be broken: but on whomsoever it shall fall, it will grind him to powder.

It is impossible for you to make such bold claims without the Word in you.

You see, it takes faith to resist the devil. Peter says it this way:

1 Peter 5:9
Whom resist steadfast in the faith...

To resist, you must stand firmly in the faith, and according to Romans 10:17, "**faith comes by hearing, and hearing by the Word of God.**" You can only resist when you know what the Word of God says about you, who you are, your position in Christ, and your consummate victory over the devil. When you have this mind in you, the devil can't do a thing to you in spiritual warfare.

Before we close this chapter, let's go back to our key verse from James chapter 4 and verse 7. There is one more thing I want you to see there.

James 4:7
Submit yourselves therefore to God. Resist the devil, and he will flee from you.

Notice what happens when you submit yourself to God and resist the devil. The Bible says he will "flee" from you. I want you to get a clear picture of what this verse is telling us, because there is something about submitting to God and resisting the devil that depicts our superiority in spiritual warfare.

The word "flee" does not simply mean to run away. It's much more vivid a description than that. It is from the Greek word *pheúgō*, and it does mean to *run away*, but it's *how* you run away that I want you to make note of. It means to *shun* or *avoid by flight something abhorrent*. It means to flee as if in terror. When you submit to God and resist the devil, you become his worst nightmare! You become dangerous, and he will do everything in his power to run away from you.

That is the truth about spiritual warfare that many Christians have not known. That is why they are busy trying to run away from the devil, or you might have a few generals that will try to fight him in spiritual warfare. But the Bible is clearly telling you that fighting is not the way to deal with the devil. You engage in spiritual warfare from a position of rest. Submitting to God—positioning yourself under the Word—by loading up your spirit with the Word, makes you aware of Christ in you. And He is at rest. He is the *real* Titanic. He is massive, a force to be reckoned with, and He cannot be moved. He is the epitome of spiritual inertia, and He is inside you, giving you the ability to fully resist the devil.

Chapter Thirteen

Mission Aborted

The Incredibles is a Pixar Animation Studios sensation about a superhero family. Because of the collateral damage caused by their superhero activities while fighting villains, they, along with all other superheroes, are banned from using their superpowers. The movie focuses primarily on the patriarch of the family, Mr Incredible, who is not adjusting well to his now mundane life. He's a forty-year-old has-been superhero living as claims adjuster Bob Parr. So, when an opportunity comes along for him to get a second shot at his superhero glory days, he jumps at the chance. The movie was a hit in every sense of the word, creating memorable characters such as Elastigirl, Violet, Dash, and Jack-Jack. And who could forget Mr Incredible's dedicated bestie and crime-fighting sidekick, Lucius Best, aka Frozone?

Tall, svelte, and consummately cool, Frozone has no real weapons to speak of except his ability to take what's inside him and use it to his advantage. This frosty superhero would use his cryokinetic skills to manipulate the water particles in him and around him and turn them into ramps of ice. The ice serves a two-fold purpose for Frozone. He uses the sheet of ice as a vehicle to get where he wants to go and throws it up as an obstacle to prevent his enemies from accomplishing their mission. Cryokinesis is not in the devil's spiritual warfare toolbox. However, he does employ Frozone-like tactics on even the most astute generals in the faith.

Apostle Paul, writing to the church at Thessalonica, expresses his longing to come and see them. This was a young church established early in his ministry, and they were under persecution. Paul, as a loving, concerned father longed to see them that he might strengthen and encourage them. But something remarkable happened. We find the account in 1 Thessalonians chapter 2, verses 17 and 18.

1 Thessalonians 2:17-18 NKJV
But we, brethren, having been taken away from you for a short time in presence, not in heart, endeavoured more eagerly to see your face with great desire. Therefore we wanted to come to you—even I, Paul, time and again—*but Satan hindered us* [emphasis added].

Now, this is Paul we're talking about, the same Paul who warned us not to be ignorant of the devil's devices.

2 Corinthians 2:11
Lest Satan should get an advantage of us: for we are not ignorant of his devices.

This was not an instance of the blind leading the blind. Paul knew what he was talking about, and if anyone was savvy to the devil's devices, it was him. How was it possible for Satan to hinder him, not once, but **"time and again?"** The only way Satan could accomplish such a feat was to use a Frozone-like military tactic called the Indirect Approach. It is the path of least resistance.

You see, Frozone was able to use ice to his advantage because ice has very little resistance. That is why an ice skater can glide across the ice without stopping. They will continue in motion unless a powerful enough force of friction causes them to stop. This corroborates with what we discussed in the previous chapter when we talked about spiritual inertia. Christ in you gives you mass, and that awareness can be increased by getting more of the Word in you. You become a heavyweight in the Spirit.

Those with greater spiritual mass cannot be easily moved by the devil in spiritual warfare. The Word in them produces so much friction, it stops the devil in his tracks. But, in the absence of resistance, the devil can use the indirect approach to manipulate circumstances to his advantage. He can hinder you as he hindered Paul. Let me show you how the devil tried to use this strategy on Jesus.

In Matthew chapter 16, Jesus is with His disciples, and He asks them a very important question. He asks, what are people saying about Me? Let's look at it in verse 13:

Matthew 16:13
When Jesus came into the coasts of Caesarea Philippi, he asked his disciples, saying, Whom do men say that I the Son of man am?

Now, this question was a set up for a revelation. Because if you continue reading, you will see that Jesus asks another question, the answer to which revealed to His disciples exactly who He was. Watch what ensues in the verses that follow.

Matthew 16:14-18
And they said, Some say that thou art John the Baptist: some, Elias; and others, Jeremias, or one of the prophets. He saith unto

them, But whom say ye that I am? And Simon Peter answered and said, Thou art the Christ, the Son of the living God. And Jesus answered and said unto him, Blessed art thou, Simon Barjona: for flesh and blood hath not revealed it unto thee, but my Father which is in heaven. And I say also unto thee, That thou art Peter, and upon this rock I will build my church; and the gates of hell shall not prevail against it.

At that moment, Peter was the favoured one. He had just received a revelation so great even Jesus exclaimed, flesh and blood did not reveal this to you. That was a tremendous and victorious experience for Peter, and unbeknownst to him, it was also a prime opportunity for the devil to attack. Paul, in 1 Corinthians 10, verse 12 says it this way:

1 Corinthians 10:12
Wherefore let him that thinketh he standeth take heed lest he fall.

I told you in an earlier chapter that one of the strategies of the devil is to attack after a great victory. That is what happened to Peter. And unfortunately, he did not yet have the spiritual mass to resist the thoughts of the devil. Watch what happens next in Matthew chapter 16, just a few verses later. Let's pick it up in verse 21:

Matthew 16:21-23
From that time forth began Jesus to shew unto his disciples, how that he must go unto Jerusalem, and suffer many things of the elders and chief priests and scribes, and be killed, and be raised again the third day. Then Peter took him, and began to rebuke him, saying, Be it far from thee, Lord: this shall not be unto thee. But he turned, and said unto Peter, Get thee behind

me, Satan: thou art an offence unto me: for thou savourest not the things that be of God, but those that be of men.

Now, I want you to catch what's happening here. Satan is really after Jesus. He wants to abort His mission, but he's still smarting from the beating he got in the wilderness when Jesus whipped him with the Word. So, rather than confront Jesus directly, he uses the indirect approach and chooses the path of least resistance, Peter.

The indirect approach was implemented by Sir Basil Liddell Hart, a British military historian and strategist. The strategy utilizes eight rules that make for very effective warfare. They are as follows:

Rule One: Adjust your ends to your means.

Rule Two: Keep your object always in mind.

Rule Three: Choose the line of the least expectation.

Rule Four: Exploit the line of least resistance.

Rule Five: Take the line of operations which offers the most alternatives.

Rule Six: Ensure both plans and dispositions are flexible.

Rule Seven: Do not throw your weight into an opponent while he is on guard.

Rule Eight: Do not renew an attack along the same lines if an attack has failed.

You can clearly see that this was the strategy Satan employed in Matthew chapter 16. It was a very strategic attack and one often used in spiritual warfare. Satan was familiar with Peter and knew how impulsive and impetuous Peter was. His very name belied his spiritual comport. Jesus, the Rock, called Peter, *Pétros*, a small stone. He did not yet have the spiritual mass to resist the devil's attack.

At that time, the other disciples weren't that much different from Peter. But what made Peter a more suitable candidate for the devil to work through was the victory Peter had just experienced. Peter had just spoken up, under the unction of the Holy Ghost, and gotten the answer right, as it were. This gave him a level of confidence (perhaps arrogance) at that moment that the others didn't have. So, when the devil planted a thought in his mind that Jesus should not go to Jerusalem and die, he met no resistance from Peter. It was the devil's thought that Peter articulated. He didn't physically hold Jesus back. But by speaking the devil's lie, he set up a roadblock with his words which Jesus promptly broke through with a rebuke.

While the strategy of indirect approach may have eight rules, in essence, it is very simple: attack the weaker to abort the mission of the stronger. The devil tried it with Jesus and failed. He later tried a similar strategy with Paul. That is why Paul said, "Satan *hindered* us."

1 Thessalonians 2:18
Therefore we wanted to come to you—even I, Paul, time and again—but Satan hindered us.

That word "hindered" is translated from the Greek word *enkóptó*, and it means to set up a *roadblock*. The objective of the hindrance is to block or delay. Paul was accustomed to these devilish tactics. That's why in 2 Corinthians 12:7, he said:

2 Corinthians 12:7
There was given to me a thorn in the flesh, the messenger of Satan to buffet me.

A lot of preachers will try to tell you that this thorn in the flesh was some physical malady that Paul had. But it tells you right there what the thorn was. Paul said it was a "messenger of Satan" that was assigned to fight against him. Messengers carry messages, and if it is a messenger of Satan, the only message it could be carrying is the devil's lies. This was a demonic spirit that was sent to plant lies in the minds of people and set them against Paul to try to hinder his progress. That is the kind of hindrance Paul faced.

Now, when you hear Paul saying, "Satan hindered us," you might think what happened to Paul was a defeat. But it actually shows the advantage Paul had and that we have over the devil in spiritual warfare. Let's look at the verse again:

1 Thessalonians 2:18
Therefore we wanted to come to you—even I, Paul, time and again—but Satan hindered us.

When reading that verse, did you ever stop to think *how* Paul knew that Satan had hindered them? The answer to that question is where the key to your victory in spiritual warfare lies. Don't think for a moment that Satan would show his hand and reveal his strategy to Paul. This was a revelation of the Holy Ghost, the same Holy Ghost who told Paul not to go into certain places. Watch what it says in Acts chapter 16, verses 6 and 7:

Acts 16:6-7
Now when they had gone throughout Phrygia and the region of Galatia, and *were forbidden of the Holy Ghost to preach the word in Asia*, After they were come to Mysia, they assayed to

go into Bithynia: *but the Spirit suffered them not* [emphasis added].

Brothers and sisters, the Holy Ghost is your secret weapon, and He doesn't play checkers. He is *The* Grandmaster of Chess. When you go to the dictionary and look up 'best chess moves,' it will tell you, *see the Holy Ghost*! He is always light years ahead of the devil. All the devil can do is react to what God is already doing. And by the time the devil gets a hint of what God is doing, he's already infinite moves behind.

The Bible calls the Holy Ghost the Wonderful Counsellor. You'll find that in Isaiah chapter 9 and verse 6.

Isaiah 9:6
His name shall be called Wonderful Counsellor...

The Holy Ghost is the Extraordinary Strategist! Hallelujah! He's the One who tells you what moves to make. He tells you where the devil is setting up His roadblocks and which way you need to take. Oh, glory be to God! As long as the Holy Spirit is around, the devil can never pull the wool over your eyes in spiritual warfare. He'll guide you through the booby traps the devil tries to set, and He'll steer you clear of every landmine.

Jesus said the Comforter—the Counsellor, the Extraordinary Strategist—will teach you all things.

John 14:26a AMPC
But the Comforter (Counselor, Helper, Intercessor, Advocate, Strengthener, Standby), the Holy Spirit, Whom the Father will

send in My name [in My place, to represent Me and act on My behalf], He will teach you all things.

He will teach you *all* things, and that includes the strategies of spiritual warfare. That's what He's doing right now as you're reading this book. He's showing you the tricks of the enemy and showing you how to deal with them. But you must develop a sensitivity to His voice, and His Voice is the Word of God.

The Bible tells us that Adam and Eve would hear the voice walking through the Garden at the cool of the day. That's Genesis 3, verse 8:

Genesis 3:8
And they heard the voice of the Lord God walking in the garden in the cool of the day

The voice of the Lord God is none other than Jesus, and Jesus is the Word. The more Word you have in you, the more sensitive you will be to the voice of the Holy Spirit. Spiritual warfare, like natural warfare, is a noisy place. There's a lot of noise in the battlefield of your mind. So, it is tantamount that you be able to distinguish His voice from every other voice.

The devil has no real weapons, just tricks. The most he can do is to try to put things in your way to try to slow you down. But you have something far superior. You have the Word and the Holy Ghost who gives you inside information. Paul said, Satan hindered us. In other words, the devil managed to get into the minds of some people around Paul and try to make it difficult for him to move around and do what he needed to do. But this is the same Paul who said, all things are working together for my good!

Romans 8:28
And we know that all things work together for good to them that love God, to them who are the called according to his purpose.

You can never be disadvantaged! You've got the Word and the Spirit, and that's an unbeatable combination in spiritual warfare. That gives you the necessary friction to stop the enemy dead in his tracks.

We are told to resist the devil. He knows those whose spiritual mass gives them the most inertia. These are the spiritually mature ones, full of the Word and aligned with the Spirit. Like Paul, they are aware of the devil's tricks and can readily resist him. But there are those whose resistance levels are low. Spiritually, they have little or no friction which makes it easier for the devil to use his tricks to manipulate them. On such ones, he utilizes the indirect approach. He avoids direct confrontation with the ones whose mission he wants to thwart and instead manipulates the weaker ones around them. By doing this, he effectually throws up obstacles that become hindrances to the ones he really wants to stop. But the Word and the Spirit will render his tactics ineffective.

In *The Incredibles*, Frozone discovers his cryokinetic abilities at a very young age. So, by the time he reaches adulthood, he's an old pro. The same is true of the devil. He's been at his scheming and trickery for a long time. He's well-practised in spiritual warfare. True enough, he is an ancient adversary. However, you still have the maximum advantage because the Ancient of Days is with you. The Bible calls Him the extraordinary strategist.

The devil is no superhero, but like every superhero, he does have an Achilles heel, something that renders him completely useless. That's something else he and Frozone have in common.

Frozone draws upon the water in his body and moisture in the air around him to activate his cryokinetic abilities. But if the air is too dry or if he's dehydrated, those abilities won't work. There is one particular scene in the movie where he finds himself surrounded by fire, trapped in a burning building, and he can't do anything at all. That is a picture of what happens when you align yourself with the Word and the Spirit in spiritual warfare.

The Bible tells us in Hebrews 12:29 that "our God is a consuming fire." In another account, Jeremiah tried to hold himself back from speaking the Word of God, but he cried out, it's like fire inside me.

Jeremiah 20:9
His word was in mine heart as a burning fire shut up in my bones.

God Himself said of His word that it is like fire. You'll find that in Jeremiah chapter 23 and verse 29:

Jeremiah 23:29
Is not my word like as a fire? saith the Lord; and like a hammer that breaketh the rock in pieces?

The Holy Spirit is also spoken of, and His power typified in terms of fire.

The Spirit and the Word will have the same effect on the devil as the hot, dry air had on Frozone. It will leave him spiritually dehydrated, and his tricks will not work. No matter what roadblocks he may try to set up to hinder you and abort your mission, it won't work. The more Word in you, the more sensitive to the Holy Spirit you will be. He is your secret weapon in spiritual warfare, and He makes you a barrier breaker to every demonic roadblock.

Chapter Fourteen

Unmasking the Devil

There's an old German proverb that says, "Fear makes the wolf bigger than he is." Fear has perpetuated the lie that the devil is powerful. That's why so many Christians are embroiled in spiritual warfare, fighting with the devil. They believe he has the power to take something away from them. It's a lie. The biggest problem you have right now is you have believed the lies of the enemy when he has told you he can get into you and that you need a deliverance minister. The devil is not as powerful as deliverance ministers have made him out to be.

It's unfortunate that our churches have become deliverance centres where ministers have become ambassadors, personal assistants, and protocol for the devil. When they are casting out devils, they put a mic in front of them to ask where they're coming from. Imagine, giving the devil a microphone that the church bought! And if you give the devil attention, he will give you direction. Listening to some ministers preach about how powerful the enemy is, you would think the devil is more powerful than God. Has it ever occurred to you that it only takes a few moments for a devil to enter a person, but it takes some deliverance ministers hours to remove it? That gives the impression that demons are more powerful than our God, which is a fabrication and a lie!

The devil is nothing more than a shadow puppet master. He holds up two fingers in front of a wall in a dark room, and you see a lion and run for cover. He depends on your darkness to make his tricks work. But all you need to do is to turn on the light, and you will see the devil for what he really is.

The Bible tells us in Psalm 119 and verse 130 that the entrance of God's Word gives us light.

Psalm 119:130
The entrance of thy words giveth light; it giveth understanding unto the simple.

The devil is not afraid of how powerfully you pray, how long your fast, or what your title is. He's afraid of light. The Word of God is a concentration of light more powerful and precise than any laser.

You need to understand that the mind is the battlefield of the devil, and there's only one thing that will cause him to be effective there, and that's darkness. The Bible warns us that it is possible for the mind to become darkened. Paul alludes to this in Ephesians chapter 4, verses 17 and 18 where it says:

Ephesians 4:17-18
This I say therefore, and testify in the Lord, that ye henceforth walk not as other Gentiles walk, in the vanity of their mind, Having the understanding darkened, being alienated from the life of God through the ignorance that is in them, because of the blindness of their heart:

149

Notice it says the understanding can be *darkened*. And Paul tells you exactly how that happens: *through ignorance*. That simply means the understanding that is darkened is deprived of the light of God's Word. A darkened mind is the breeding ground for fear and spiritual warfare. The problem is simple: you lack accurate information.

The Bible says the enemy was defeated. If Jesus defeated the devil—and He did—what are you doing fighting him? It's a very simple thing. Paul said, **"the weapons of our warfare are not carnal"** (2 Corinthians 10:4). Many Christians get confused when they see the word 'warfare.' It's not what you think it is. It is from the Greek word *strateia* from which we get the word *strategies*. It's all about strategies. It has nothing to do with fighting anyone.

Somebody says, *but the Bible says we wrestle not*. Let me take you to the scriptures so you can understand precisely what this wrestling is all about. Ephesians chapter 6, verse 12 reads like this:

Ephesians 6:12
For we wrestle...

Let's stop right there. The word that talks about wrestling there is the word *pálē*, and it relates to an ancient form of wrestling from the Roman empire.

In those days, there was a boxing sport called Pankration, meaning "with all might or force." There were no rounds, no boxing gloves and no time limit. Both men were naked, and there were only three rules: no gouging out your opponent's eyes, no biting, and you were not allowed to attack the genitals. Everything else was fair game. They used to say death was the only way you could retire from boxing, that's how dangerous it was. Pankration allowed the use of weapons. But when it came to wrestling, the only thing needed was stamina. That is why in Ephesians 6, verses 12 and 13, Paul begins his discourse with wrestling but ends with standing.

Ephesians 6:12, 13b
For we wrestle not against flesh and blood, but against principalities, against powers, against the rulers of the darkness of this world, against spiritual wickedness in high places... And having done all, to stand.

Wrestling has nothing to do with fighting.

Christians are fighting the devil every day, and Jesus is wondering, what did I accomplish on the cross? Did Jesus die for nothing, so that you can resist the devil all night? Did He die just so you can do four weeks of fasting to get one simple job that a sinner gets without praying? A thousand times, no! Yet, there are still people who are convinced that they need deliverance. Am I saying demons can't get into people? I'm saying they can, but they get into ignorant people. We deliver people in the church, but the people we deliver are fools whose minds are darkened through ignorance.

If you only knew what the devil is, you would never fear him. My man of God, Pastor Chris said, when I saw the devil the first time, I came up with one conclusion, he's empty. He said, I thought that I could find something, but there was nothing in it. *There are Christians who fear the very name 'devil,' yet it's not even a name.*

151

The word 'devil' comes from the Greek word diábolos which is a compound of the words dia and balló. Now, dia means to *go all the way through* or *to pierce something from one side all the way through to the other side*. And the word *balló* means to *throw consistently with a purpose*, like when you throw a dart or a stone. It's the same word that Jesus used in John chapter 8, verse 7 when He confronted the accusers of the woman who was caught in the act of adultery. He said:

John 8:7
So when they continued asking him, he lifted up himself, and said unto them, He that is without sin among you, let him first cast a stone at her.

The word translated "cast" there is the Greek word *balló*. So, you have *dia* and *balló*, and when you join these two words together, you get *diábolos* which means *to repetitiously throw something— striking again and again and again until the object being struck has finally been completely penetrated*. That is what the devil does. His strategy is to wear out the saints by bombarding their minds with the fiery darts of his lies until he pierces through. Daniel chapter 7, verse 25 says it this way:

Daniel 7:25a
And he shall speak great words against the most High, *and shall wear out the saints* [emphasis added] of the most High

The Hebrew word there for "wear out" is *blá*. Interestingly enough, it has a pronunciation almost identical to the Greek word *balló*. The Hebrew meaning is to *wear out by harassing constantly*. And, watch this, it is only used in a *mental sense*. That tells you precisely what the job description of the devil is. His job is to constantly harass your mind, striking again and again, until he pierces through with his lies.

So when you say 'devil,' all you are saying is *the one who throws consistently until he pierces through*. It's not a name. It's a job description. Imagine picking up the classifieds section of the newspaper and running away because of a job description you see printed there. That's absurd! Yet there are Christians who are running away from the 'devil,' which is nothing more than a job description.

When you see 'devil' it's telling you how the adversary operates: *he assaults the mind*. He constantly tells you one lie after the other. He keeps on striking with the objective of wearing down the resistance of the one being assaulted until he pierces through and gets his lies in there. That is what he attempted to do to Jesus in the wilderness. He kept on tempting Jesus over and over until Jesus said, "It is said…" (Luke 4:12). Then the Bible says the devil left Jesus for a season.

Luke 4:13
And when the devil had ended all the temptation, he departed from him for a season.

That means the devil had every intention of coming back at a more opportune time to continue his mental assault. Why? Because he's diábolos. He is consistently throwing. He can never tire. Even with Jesus he said, you won this time, but I'm coming back.

If there is anything you can learn from the devil it's that he's consistent and persistent. We must also be consistent and persistent so that the Word can prevail over his tactics. The Bible says, so mightily grew the word of God and prevailed in Ephesus.

Acts 19:20
So mightily grew the word of God and prevailed.

Now, I don't know whether you know where Ephesus is. It's Turkey. Imagine how many Muslims are in Turkey right now, and the Bible says, one guy called Paul caused the Word of God to grow mightily in Turkey. It prevailed over Islam, prevailed over any religion. One man made the Word prevail. The fact that he made the Word prevail implies that no prevailing would take place unless there was a continuous loading of the Word. In other words, there was a level at which the Word was so little that it could not prevail.

So God is also consistent and persistent. The devil only copies. He's a fake, but you are the real imitators of God. That is why it is paramount that you be consistent and persistent about flooding your spirit with the light of God's Word. Otherwise, your ignorance will cause you to believe that you are vulnerable, cursed, and in need of deliverance. The truth is, you don't need deliverance. What you need is to get the Word into you.

Now I want you to see something here that I keep saying to some of our fellow-ministers who like removing demons from people. It's like that's all they do: Deliverance Sunday; Breakthrough Sunday. After you breakthrough, you need another breakthrough to breakthrough the other breakthrough. It just happens like that, over and over again, a cycle. And so many people like all this laying on of hands, and oil poured on them until they smell like sunflower oil. All because they believe they need some kind of deliverance. It's unfortunate.

The Bible tells us something very interesting in Proverbs chapter 26 and verse 2. It reads this way:

Proverbs 26:2
As the bird by wandering, as the swallow by flying, so the curse causeless shall not come.

In other words, a curse you don't deserve will fly away from you. It is a causeless curse. No child of God is cursed or deserves to be cursed. But what that is telling you is that when you don't know that you are not cursed and cannot be cursed, there are things you can do out of ignorance (thinking that you are cursed) that break the hedge of protection encompassing your life. That mindset wears down your resistance and makes it easy for the devil's lies to pierce through. It is your belief that you are cursed that allows the enemy to infiltrate your mind and perpetuate the lie that you already believe.

Can you see that it is not the devil who has the power to hurt you? It is your own ignorance. The Bible says he that breaks the hedge the serpent will bite him. Ignorance of the Word of God opens your life up to trouble and gives the adversary the opportunity to work.

It is your duty to see to it that the Word of God prevails in your life. Jesus said it this way in Luke 11 and verse 35:

Luke 11:35
Take heed therefore that the light which is in thee be not darkness.

155

And the psalmist said, the entrance of Thy word gives light. That's Psalm 119, verse 130:

Psalm 119:130
The entrance of Thy words giveth light; it giveth understanding unto the simple.

There is no way you can remain ignorant and foolish when you are filled with the Word of God. It's impossible for you to be in darkness. The light of God is the Word of God, so the more Word you have in you, the more light you have. That is the strength of your defence system and what makes you terrifying to the devil.

The Bible says faith comes from hearing and hearing by the Word of God. That means faith is a product of knowledge. Faith is for the intelligent. People say, but I have a lot of faith. You don't. When you don't have knowledge, you don't have faith. People think faith is some kind of feeling: I feel; I believe God; I trust Him. Yet these same people will turn around and say, I don't know why things are not happening for me. You have made God a liar. God says if you have faith, it works.

1 John 5, verse 4 tells us that it is our faith that causes us to overcome.

1 John 5:4
For whatsoever is born of God overcometh the world: and this is the victory that overcometh the world, even our faith.

That word "even" means exactly our faith. That means when you have faith, nothing is impossible. The moment you see your situation as being impossible, you don't have faith. I don't care how convinced you are that you have it. Faith is a product of knowledge. How much Word do you have in you that you have converted into knowledge? That knowledge becomes your speech, an aggregate of what is inside. That's why Jesus said, I speak to you, but you can't understand My speech because you don't have My words (John 8:43). That means whatever comes out of my mouth is an aggregate of what is in my spirit.

Now, watch what Paul says. He says, "**for we are not ignorant of his devices**" (2 Corinthians 2:11). If he says we are not ignorant of his devices, that means the devil only has tricks. He has no power to defeat anybody. The power the devil has is the one we give him. How does that happen? As he consistently throws and begins to pierce through, you agree with his lies. Let me give you an example.

Have you ever been sick, and you start declaring the Name of Jesus over your sickness? *In the Name of Jesus, I decree and declare...* and then the pain gets even stronger. The throbbing is even more intense. The more you call the Name of Jesus, the more pain you feel until you say, *Oh, why me, Jesus?* Aha! That's when the devil has gotten you where he wants you. He has managed to pierce through.

Do you remember the story of Job? The devil and God were in Heaven discussing Job, but Job is not involved in the discussions. This is a meeting to which only God and the devil are privy. And God says, have you checked out my servant, a man who runs away from evil. God says, I'm convinced Job will never do anything against Me, but the devil was not convinced. That means Job had

157

managed to convince God, but he had not managed to convince the devil. So faith, when it's full in knowledge, has to get to a point where you convince the devil you will never change.

Look at Ulf Ekman. He was the pastor of one of the largest Pentecostal churches in Scandinavia and the founder of Livets Ord (Word of Life). He is noted as being the one responsible for bringing the Word of Faith charismatic movement to Scandinavia. Powerful! The man would stand in front, and people would fall under the power. Miracles would take place. Then one night, he called his secretary and told her, the church is no longer mine; I'm not coming back. I'm now a member of the Roman Catholic church.

When you see founders walk away from their own churches just like that, that is the work of *diábolos continually assaulting the mind.* He keeps on doing it, pounding and pounding away, until one day you say, I give up. The moment you start considering what the devil is saying, he keeps on going until he pierces through and you agree.

Remember, even God admits the devil is intelligent. After all, He once was Lucifer, a being created by God. Not only is he intelligent, but he is also experienced. Before you were born, he was there messing up your great grandfather. He knows exactly what to say when you stand against him. He's full of strategies. But, the weapons of our warfare are not carnal but mighty through God to the pulling down of strongholds. You have what it takes to stop his assault on your mind. You and the Word form a united front that pushes the enemy back where he belongs.

Let me repeat this for the record. I'm by no means saying demons are not real. Neither am I saying deliverance is not necessary. Deliverance is necessary for the ignorant people that have demons. My bone of contention is with the minister who talks about deliverance continually without teaching people how to stay delivered. How come the people that deliver other people don't have any videos where we can see these deliverance ministers being delivered themselves? If they can't be possessed, why aren't they telling people how not to be possessed? Because one thing ministers know is this, if they deliver you and tell you the secret for self-deliverance, you won't attend church. That's why deliverance ministers will tell you, come to church for twelve weeks, and if you miss one deliverance session, we start over.

I am a deliverance minister. I deliver the Word. That is the key to deliverance that Paul gave us in Ephesians chapter 6. Let's look at verses 14 through 16 again.

Ephesians 6:14-16
Stand therefore, having your loins girt about with truth, and having on the breastplate of righteousness; And your feet shod with the preparation of the gospel of peace; Above all, taking the shield of faith, wherewith ye shall be able to quench all the fiery darts of the wicked.

He says, "**stand therefore, having your loins girt about with truth**." What is truth? Jesus said I am the Truth. And Jesus, according to Revelation 19:13, is the Word. So your loins are girded with Jesus who is the Word.

Then he says, "**having the breastplate of righteousness**." The Bible says Jesus is our righteousness, and Jesus is the Word. So we're still on the Word. Let's go on. "**And your feet shod with the preparation of the gospel**." What is the Gospel? It's the Word! He then says, "**above all, taking the shield of faith**." According to Romans 10, verse 17, faith comes by hearing and hearing by the Word of God. So, we are still on the Word. Are you getting it?

Paul continues, "**wherewith you shall be able to quench all the fiery darts of the wicked**—not some, but *all*. Notice, *diábolos is* the one who throws to the extent of piercing through. If he is piercing through, it means he's using darts. Paul says if you don't want these darts to pierce through, use the Word! Your pastor told you it's spiritual warfare. This is a Word fight. It has nothing to do with anything else. The devil uses lies, his words, and you've got to use God's Word!

When you understand who the devil is, you realize immediately that he is utterly defeated. And remember, a war is between two undefeated champions or undefeated enemies. Once one is defeated, it's no longer a war. It's one person who was beaten trying to claim they were not. That's all the devil is doing. He's trying to convince you that he can still fight. And the day you believe that, he gets a foothold because he knows you believe that he's still powerful.

The devil cannot work without your permission. That's how powerless and empty he is. But he uses clever tactics. He will contort the face of the person that he possesses to try to put fear in you. He will employ any strategy he can to convince you that he has power.

I remember one such occasion when I was in St. Lucia. After I cast the demon out of this one particular lady, she fell as if dead. They checked her pulse, and they couldn't find it. I told them, when I land in Britain, that's when she'll come out of this stupor. I got to Britain, went past the immigration and got in my car, then the phone rang. They said she has just come back.

I know of a man, I will not say the name, but I know him. When he was just starting out in ministry, one night, in the middle of the night, the devil came into his room like wind. All the windows opened at once. Curtains were flying everywhere. Chairs were shaking, and all the furniture was getting rearranged. The man woke up, turned on the light, and looked around in surprise. The place was all messed up. But the moment the man said, in the Name of Jesus, the windows not only closed but latched shut. The man realized the furniture was still out of place. So, he got out of bed, opened the windows again and said, devil, come back, and put the furniture back like you found it!

The devil is a nameless nobody. He is *diábolos,* the John Doe of the spiritual realm. But I will say one thing, he makes a great maid. He put the furniture back nicely and cleaned even the parts that were not cleaned before.

Chapter Fifteen

Winning

Casting out devils is not deliverance. I know I just messed up your theology right there, so let me repeat. Casting out devils is *not* deliverance. It is vacancy. In fact, many deliverance ministers, due to their neglect and selfish unconcern, are spiritual residential real estate developers and interior designers for devils. They specialize in creating places for demons to reside.

That is what Jesus was talking about in Matthew chapter 12, verses 43 to 45 when He said:

Matthew 12:43-45
When the unclean spirit is gone out of a man, he walketh through dry places, seeking rest, and findeth none. Then he saith, I will return into my house from whence I came out; and when he is come, he findeth it empty, swept, and garnished. Then goeth he, and taketh with himself seven other spirits more wicked than himself, and they enter in and dwell there: and the last state of that man is worse than the first. Even so shall it be also unto this wicked generation.

You see, it's not enough to only cast devils out. That only leaves a vacancy. And if that vacancy is not filled with the Spirit and the Word of God, the Bible says, "**the last state of that man is worse than the first**." So, all of these deliverance ministers, going around casting out devils but not teaching the Word of God and telling people how they can remain free, are doing a disservice to those who are tormented by devils. It is tantamount to stripping them naked and serving them on a platter to the enemy. It would be better for them if these preachers left them with their one devil than to set them up for eight.

Deliverance without the Word will deliver you to the enemy. That is what was happening to the church at Ephesus. They were under spiritual attack because, in their ignorance, they were giving place to the devil and grieving the Holy Spirit. The devil had penetrated. So, Paul had to teach the Ephesians how the devil operates and how to stand against him.

Twice in Ephesians chapter 6, Paul tells the church to put on the whole armour of God. In verse 11, he says:

Ephesians 6:11
Put on the whole armour of God…

Then again in verse 13, he repeats the instruction and says:

Ephesians 6:13
Wherefore take unto you the whole armour of God

At first glance, it appears that Paul is saying the same thing. But a closer examination of the text gives us a subtle and crucial distinction.

"Take unto you" is the Greek compound word *analambánō*, which finds its roots in the words *ana* and *lambánō*. Now, watch this. Ana means to *repeat the action* or *do it like you once did*, and lambánō means to *take right now* or *to take with urgency or force.* So, what was Paul saying? He was telling them that they had dropped their spiritual weaponry. They were no longer walking in the power of the Word of God. They were now operating in the flesh. So Paul says, get back in the Word like you once were and do it now!

I want you to understand that Ephesus was the most Bible taught church at the time, but they were naked before the enemy. They had not matured. As a result, the devil had found his way into the church, and on a practical level, they were losing the battle. So, Paul writes to them and says, "finally my brethren" (Ephesians 6:10).

Now, when Paul says "finally," he is not suggesting that spiritual warfare is a topic that should be prioritized above all else. That is the problem some churches are having right now. They have made the devil and spiritual warfare the priority of their ministry, even above God and His Word. Paul was simply saying, in light of what is going on in the church at Ephesus, I'm about to tell you something. And if you don't remember anything else, remember this. And then he tells them about spiritual warfare. That was the subject he needed to address because the church then, as it does now, needed to know how the devil operates and how to take authority over him.

Paul expounds on five different words that are essential for you to understand when it comes to the subject of spiritual warfare. When you understand these five words, you will know how the devil operates, and you will be able to undo what he's trying to do to you. The first word you need to understand is the word "devil" that we find in Ephesians chapter 6 and verse 11:

Ephesians 6:11
Put on the whole armour of God, that ye may be able to stand against the wiles of the devil.

He says, in spiritual warfare, you need to stand against the wiles of the "devil," *diábolos. The first thing you need to be mindful of is that 'devil' is not a name, it's a job description. It describes how the devil functions. Diábolos* repetitiously and persistently strikes until he penetrates the object. That is why the word devil is sometimes translated as slanderer. *Diábolos* is one who brings slanderous accusations. He hurls lies and insults over and over again with the intention to *dia*, pierce through. His objective is to penetrate the mind with his lies.

Throughout the New Testament, every place where the words war and warfare are used, it is always in connection with the mind. The devil knows the mind is the central control centre for your life. If he can seize the mind, then he can affect what you think and believe. If he can affect what you think, he will dominate your emotions, which in turn will affect all your relationships and your entire life. Understand that the primary arena for warfare is the mind.

Then, Paul wants us to know that this diábolos has "wiles." That's the second word. The wiles of the devil are his *methodeía or* his *tricks*. It is the word from which we get the word method. This is another compound word consisting of the root words *metá* and *hodós*. I want you to catch this. *Metá* means *with*, and *hodós* means *a road or avenue*. So, it describes the devil operating on a road of attack. Roads go somewhere. They have a destination. So the devil knows where he's going, and the destination he has in mind is your mind.

The devil plays mind games. That's why in 2 Corinthians chapter 2, and verse 11, Paul says:

2 Corinthians 2:11
For we are not ignorant of his *devices* [emphasis added].

"Devices" is the third word. The word "devices" comes from the Greek word *nóēma,* which is from the root word *noûs*, meaning *mind.* So, the devil's modus operandi is to mess up your mind so that you can't think straight. It is no longer thinking correctly. His purpose is to penetrate the mind and fill it with lies and false ideas until it becomes confused. When that happens, you have a "stronghold." That's word number four.

2 Corinthians 10 and verse 4 puts it this way:

2 Corinthians 10:4
For the weapons of our warfare are not carnal, but mighty through God to the pulling down of strong holds.

Now, that word "stronghold" is translated from the Greek word *ochýrōma*, which describes either a *fortress* or *prison*. The devil, *diábolos,* assaults and penetrates the mind so that it no longer believes the truth. When that door opens, the devil gets in and builds a stronghold, a *fortress.*

A fortress has tall walls and is designed to be impenetrable. It is also a place where a king lives. So, the devil operates by moving in or occupying the mind with his lies. Then from this lofty position in our minds, he begins to dictate what we believe, what we think, what we say, whether or not we're going to get well, whether our marriage will get better, and everything else about our lives. That stronghold then becomes a prison. You look out and wish to be free, but you don't know how to get free. You are imprisoned.

That leads us to "oppression," our fifth word. We see this word in Acts chapter 10 and verse 38, where it says:

Acts 10:38
How God anointed Jesus of Nazareth with the Holy Ghost and with power: who went about doing good, and healing all that were *oppressed* [emphasis added] of the devil; for God was with Him.

That word "oppressed" means to be tyrannized by a wicked king. It depicts the devil cruelly ruling over people, manipulating and controlling them.

The *Devil* uses *wiles* to operate on a road with your mind as the destination. He then employs *devices* to scramble and confuse you with mind games so that you believe a lie. That belief allows him to set up a *stronghold*, a prison in the mind, which results in *oppression*. Then the devil moves in like a tyrant to rule, dominate and manipulate your life. But there is a way to head him off at the pass.

In 2 Corinthians 10, verse 5, Paul tells us that when the devil tries to move in and set up a stronghold in your mind, you must cast down his "imaginations," *logismós*. There are two kinds of imaginations or vain thoughts: logical and illogical. Both of these can be strongholds.

An illogical stronghold is something that is untrue, but because you hear it over and over again, you start to believe and embrace it. And what you embrace is what you manifest. But sometimes the devil speaks through common sense. It's logical. For example, the devil can appeal to your logical mind to create doubt. Let's say, for example, that you want to start a business. The devil will step in and tell you that you don't have the money to start, or your skillset is insufficient, or you don't have the time to start a business. These are all logical reasons. And if you listen to them long enough, a logical stronghold can imprison you. In both cases, you've got to deal with them in the same way: cast them down.

Understand that you've got two voices speaking to you all the time. You have the voice of God which is His Word, and His Word is truth. If you listen to truth, truth will build a truthful stronghold in your life and build a truthful fortress in your mind. That truth will dominate you and you'll believe it, and what you believe will manifest as your reality. But the voice of the devil is also talking to you telling you lies, trying to build a fortress in your mind. If you listen to that voice, he'll build that fortress in your mind, you'll believe it, and that will become your reality. The voice you listen to determines what will become your reality.

So, the Bible says that we are to pull down strongholds, cast down imaginations and everything that stands against the knowledge of God.

2 Corinthians 10:4b-5
Pulling down of strong holds; Casting down imaginations, and every high thing that exalteth itself against the knowledge of God.

The knowledge of God is what the Word of God says about you. He says you're righteous. He says you're rich. He says you're prosperous, whole and healthy. Anything that goes against what God says about you *must be pulled down*. And you can only do that if you are filled with the knowledge of God's Word.

So, you understand how the devil operates. But also understand God has given you the power and armour to stand against the wiles of the devil. Let God's Word release its power in your life. We have more authority and power than the devil. The Bible says, greater is He that is in us, than he that is in the world (1 John 4:4). Remember, all the devil has is tricks.

You may wonder why it seems the devil is winning so many victories. There is a simple explanation. The devil has something the Church often does not have, commitment, organization, and discipline. The Church can't even decide if they are going to show up for Sunday service; they battle with submitting to their pastor, and they struggle to read their Bible. When the Church matches the commitment, organization, and discipline the devil has, we will put him to flight. We have the mind of Christ, the Word of

God, and the power of the Holy Ghost. We are well equipped. Now we need to be committed, organized, and disciplined.

You have the power and the authority to stand against the devil. You, the Word, and the Spirit form a united front that pushes the enemy out of your territory and down where he belongs. That's why Paul in Ephesians 6, verse 13 says,

Ephesians 6:13
And having done all, to stand.

This is not standing and enduring. No! If you try to stand and take what the devil dishes out, he will beat the daylights out of you. That's not what Paul is saying. He means, having brought everything to its ultimate conclusion, stand. It's the picture of you at the end of the fight—not your fight, the devil's. You will be the one who is standing. That's God's prophetic declaration that you are already ordained to be the last man standing.

You're not going to win, you've already won, and you're equipped for any foe. The Word of God in you makes you an unconquerable opponent. The Word of God is the skin from which the leather of the belt of truth is cut. It is the metal from which the breastplate of righteousness is forged. It is what gives traction to the shoes of the preparation of the Gospel of peace.

The Word is the conveyor of the shield of faith and the water with which it is saturated to quench all the fiery darts of the wicked. It is the preserving power that protects your mind from the battle axe of the enemy. The Word is the rhema that provides strategic intelligence to outwit the enemy and gives wings to our prayers of intercession for all the saints.

The unadulterated Word gives us the assurance that as we give to the man and woman of God for the furtherance of the Kingdom, all our needs will be met in abundance. The Word of God is the warp and woof of the whole armour of God that makes us unparalleled champions over anything the devil throws our way.

Chapter Sixteen

Unusual Strategies

Warfare has absolutely nothing to do with war or fighting, so put your fists down. We read words like warfare, weapons, and wrestle, and we immediately associate them with something physical. But this warfare is not about anything physical. The Bible tells us this in 2 Corinthians chapter 10 and verse 4:

2 Corinthians 10:4
For the weapons of our warfare are not carnal, but mighty through God to the pulling down of strong holds

That is one of the foundational verses that deals with the subject of spiritual warfare. So, our understanding of what Paul is talking about is imperative.

Paul uses the word "warfare," and that word has to do with a military commander, which is not you. Let me say it plainly. You are *not* the military commander in spiritual warfare. I know there are generals out there who believe that they are called to be commanders in spiritual warfare and deliverance. But when I show you what "warfare" really means, you will either get in line with the real military commander or continue with your delusions of grandeur.

By choosing to use this word "warfare," the Holy Spirit through Paul clues us in on some vital information about spiritual warfare.

Now, the term "warfare" is translated from the Greek word *strateía*, which is comprised of two Greek words: *stratos* meaning *an encamped army*, and *agó* meaning to *lead, move* and *guide*. So, the accurate depiction of warfare, as Paul describes it, is of an encamped army that is led, moved, and guided. In fact, *strateía* is the word from which we derive the word *strategy*. Warfare, therefore, is not about fighting. It's about the *strategy* of the military commander.

Paul says that we must stand against the wiles—the methodeía— of *the devil, his tricks.* Wiles describes the strategies or plans of the devil. He is not haphazard about what he does. He develops a strategy to attack. But remember, the devil is only reactive. He couldn't come up with an original idea if you paid him. He simply reacts to what God is doing or has already done. So, when you see the devil using strategies, all he is doing is trying to copy what God is already doing. And you'll soon see that the devil is not the only one with a few tricks up his sleeve.

The Power of Strategy

The Holy Spirit is the Master Strategist. The Bible calls Him Wonderful Counsellor, which means the Extraordinary Strategist. He operates on the highest level, and He knows what you don't know. Therefore, He may tell you to do something that seems strange to you at first. But if you will listen to the Holy Spirit, He will give you a strategy that is superior to any schemes of the devil.

You see, the problem with the devil is he is the prince of darkness. He is ignorant of all the facts. That's why he will go for buckshot rather than a single bullet. He tries to cover more territory because he doesn't have all the intel to launch a more precise attack. We saw an example of this when the devil went after Eve in the Garden of Eden. He came to Eve and said, "did God say you shouldn't eat from *every* tree?" (see Genesis chapter 3, verse 1). He was trying to get information about what God said. He didn't know. When you see him pulling out big guns, it's not that he's so powerful. It's that he has to try to cover a large area in hopes that he might hit his target. That was what he did when he implemented the Herod strategy.

The Bible lets us know in Matthew chapter 2 that when Jesus was born, a man named Herod was king of Judaea. It says that wise men came from the East looking for baby Jesus so that they could worship Him. They asked around to find out where is He that is born King of the Jews. When the devil got wind of this, it made him very nervous. So, he accesses the mind of Herod and plants the thought to kill Jesus.

So, Herod calls for these wise men, and he tries to trick them into leading him to where baby Jesus was. He lies to them and tells them when you find Him, let me know where He is so that I can come and worship Him too. The Herod strategy was designed to snuff out the young life of Jesus. But because he had no idea who Jesus was, he went after all the male children two years old and under. Little did he know the Holy Ghost had an unusual strategy of His own.

God already knew what the devil was planning to do. So, He gives Joseph a strategy for preserving the life of Jesus from the devil's

Herod strategy. And this was the strategy: *run*! Matthew chapter 2, verse 13 tells us:

Matthew 2:13
And when they were departed, behold, the angel of the Lord appeareth to Joseph in a dream, saying, Arise, and take the young child and his mother, *and flee* [emphasis added] into Egypt, and be thou there until I bring thee word: for Herod will seek the young child to destroy him.

Now, just think about that for a moment. God is omnipotent, that means He is all-powerful. Yet He can give you a strategy to run away from the devil's strategy, and it doesn't have anything to do with cowardice. Why would an all-powerful God tell you to run? It is because running can be a strategy of the Extraordinary Strategist.

If Joseph had not obeyed the voice of the Holy Ghost when He told him to take the child and flee, Herod would have killed Jesus. That may seem hard to believe because we think that the life of Christ was indestructible. But if that were the case, God would not have warned Joseph to take the child and flee. Additionally, the Holy Spirit was already working a strategy to fulfil the scripture where God said, I have called my son out of Egypt.

Matthew 2:14-15
When he arose, he took the young child and his mother by night, and departed into Egypt: And was there until the death of Herod: *that it might be fulfilled which was spoken of the Lord by the prophet, saying, Out of Egypt have I called my son* [emphasis added].

Why would God tell someone to run from what the devil is doing? It's a strategy. When God tells you to run, it is to place you in a more advantageous position. It is never a fear-based instruction. It is a strategic instruction to position you out of the way of danger. Did He not say in Psalm 91, verse 3 that when the devil tries to mess you up, He will deliver you from the traps the enemy tries to set for you?

Psalm 91:3
Surely he shall deliver thee from the snare of the fowler, and from the noisome pestilence.

That kind of deliverance is not the kind of deliverance you see taking place in many churches. This is a divine instruction that will snatch you away from the trap *before* you get to it. Fleeing at the instruction of the Holy Ghost is a divine *strategy*.

Many Christians, young and old, end up in compromising, dangerous, even life-threatening situations because they try to fight instead of running away when God tells them to. And the devil is implementing the same Herod strategy that he tried to use to destroy the Christ child before He had a chance to mature and grow up. You see, the devil is not really after you: he's after the same thing now as he was back then. He's not really attacking you; he's attacking the Christ in you because He wants to keep Christ from being fully formed in you.

Sometimes we help the devil do this, especially when it comes to areas that deal with our flesh. We fool ourselves into thinking, I can handle this, or I know how far to go before I pull back. But don't fool yourself. Your flesh is never converted, so don't put any confidence in it. Sometimes Christians allow pride to lure them into fights that they were never supposed to fight, and then they wonder why the devil seems to be winning. Too many Christians spend too much time fighting the devil when these fights could be avoided if they would simply follow the strategy of the Holy Ghost and run away when He instructs them to.

Running does not mean that you're a coward or that you're not able to stand your ground. You are able! But running when God says to run means you have received a divine instruction, and you have matured enough in the faith to be able to recognise when not to fight. There were several times in Jesus' life when He chose to run, situations that He knew would endanger His life or ministry. How much more should we run away when God tells us to? It's a divine strategy!

To flee means to escape, to avoid or shun completely. It means to run away. Part of the reason many Christians end up in fights with the devil is that they stay close enough to him for him to be able to take a swing at them. Then, when he strikes and pierces through, they call it persecution. That's not persecution. That's you getting into a mess because you didn't listen to the voice of God and follow His strategy.

When God says run, that's not the time to pray. When God says run, that's not the time to speak in tongues. When God says run, that's not the time to make declarations. When God says run, *run*! If you don't run when God says to run, you've already given the devil an advantage because now you are functioning out of disobedience. You have left yourself wide open for the devil to attack and pierce through.

177

God's strategy may not always make sense. It may even seem foolish. But as the Bible says, the foolishness of God is wiser than man. That's what Paul tells us in 1 Corinthians 1, verse 25:

1 Corinthians 1:25
Because the foolishness of God is wiser than men; and the weakness of God is stronger than men.

In the book of Joshua, chapter 6, verses 1 through 21, we see another example of divine strategy used at the battle of Jericho. The account begins in chapter 5, where Joshua has an encounter with the Military Commander. The Bible calls Him the Captain of the Lord of Hosts. Now, watch what it says in Joshua chapter 5, verses 13 to 15:

Joshua 5:13-15
And it came to pass, when Joshua was by Jericho, that he lifted up his eyes and looked, and, behold, there stood a man over against him with his sword drawn in his hand: and Joshua went unto him, and said unto him, Art thou for us, or for our adversaries? And he said, Nay; but as captain of the host of the Lord am I now come. And Joshua fell on his face to the earth, and did worship, and said unto him, What saith my Lord unto his servant? And the captain of the Lord's host said unto Joshua, Loose thy shoe from off thy foot; for the place whereon thou standest is holy. And Joshua did so.

The Commander gives Joshua a divine strategy that does not require any of the children of Israel to lift even a finger fighting the enemy. The first thing the Bible tells us is that the victory belonged to the children of Israel before they did anything. Jericho was already defeated. Verse 2 of Joshua chapter 6 says it this way:

Joshua 6:2
And the Lord said unto Joshua, See, I have given into thine hand Jericho, and the king thereof, and the mighty men of valour.

There was no fight involved in this warfare, only an unusual strategy. God says all I want you to do is to march around the city of Jericho and have a praise party. The Lord told Joshua to gather his soldiers and march around the city for six days. The instructions were explicit. Seven priests were to go in front blowing their trumpets, followed by priests carrying the Ark of the Covenant. Some of the soldiers were to go in front of the priests who were blowing the trumpets. Some were to follow behind the priests who were carrying the Ark. No one was to say a word. Just march around once while the priests continually blew their trumpets, then return to the camp. They did this for six days.

On the seventh day, the strategy was for them to do the same thing they had done for the past six days but with a slight twist. This time, they would march around Jericho seven times, and on the seventh time, they would shout for joy. That was the strategy. And when they followed it, the Bible says, the walls of the enemy came tumbling down.

Joshua 6:20
So the people shouted when the priests blew with the trumpets: and it came to pass, when the people heard the sound of the trumpet, and the people shouted with a great shout, that the wall fell down flat, so that the people went up into the city, every man straight before him, and they took the city.

God's strategy does not have to make sense to you. But if you follow it, it will work every time, and you will never have to fight.

You see, the Holy Spirit is so brilliant that He can allow the devil to strategise without realising that his devilish strategy is just a tiny part of God's strategy. God's strategy is always to start from the winning side and work backwards, putting things in place and allowing things to happen that support His plan. His strategies are always pre-emptive. The devil, on the other hand, can only work from the losing side. Such was the case when the devil tried to kill Jesus before He got to the cross.

Watch what Jesus says in Luke chapter 13, verse 33:

Luke 13:33
Nevertheless I must walk to day, and to morrow, and the day following: for it cannot be that a prophet perish out of Jerusalem.

Everything Jesus did while on the earth was part of God's divine strategy. Dying on the cross was part of that strategy, and Jesus, fulfilling prophecy, knew that it had to happen in Jerusalem. So He said, I can't die outside Jerusalem, and by the unction of the Holy Spirit, He implemented a strange strategy. He told his disciples to go and buy swords. Look at what He says in Luke chapter 22, verses 35 through 37:

Luke 22:35-37
And He said unto them, When I sent you without purse, and scrip, and shoes, lacked ye any thing? And they said, Nothing. Then said He unto them, But now, he that hath a purse, let him take it, and likewise his scrip: and *he that hath no sword, let him*

sell his garment, and buy one [emphasis added]. **For I say unto you, that this that is written must yet be accomplished in me [*strategy,* emphasis added], And he was reckoned among the transgressors: for the things concerning me have an end.**

Jesus was implementing a divine pre-emptive strategy knowing the devil's strategy was to kill Him before He got to the cross.

In 1 Thessalonians chapter 2 and verse 18, we see another unusual strategy implemented. Paul says:

1 Thessalonians 2:18
Wherefore we would have come unto you, even I Paul, once and again; but Satan hindered us.

The devil's strategy was to hinder Paul. He could not hinder Paul directly because Paul had too much spiritual mass for the devil to tangle with. So, he had to work through people around Paul to try to slow him down. It might have been the ruler of the city that barred them from entering. But since Paul was not ignorant of the devil's devices, he used another strategy, realising that the ruler wasn't working on his own but was part of the devil's strategy. Little did the devil know that his hindering strategy was part of God's divine strategy. Watch what happens.

The reason why we read in the Bible that the devil "hindered us" is that part was included in Paul's strategy, *a letter*. Paul realised he was hindered by one strategy of the enemy, and he didn't stop and say we'll try again tomorrow. He changed strategy, and instead of trying to enter the city, he made the letter his strategy instead. He achieved even more with a letter than he would have done in person, because, in those days, letters were sent to various churches to be read. That is why you'll find Paul saying, "when this letter is read to you, send it also to…"

Even though Paul was prevented from entering a city, his letter travelled where he could not and got even better results than if he had gone in person. If Paul had delivered the message himself, it could have been misquoted as it was passed along by word of mouth to other churches. But the letter carried all the words of Paul and could be conveyed intact and read with accuracy.

I had a similar experience to Paul where I was hindered from entering Zambia. The wife of the president met me at the airport to prevent me from entering the country. I had a work visa, and everything was in order. But the president was scared that I might endorse the opposition leader, which I had no intention of doing since politics is below my pay grade.

The whole Parliament sat to discuss my imminent arrival, and the president decided my entering the country was a no-no. So, even with a visa, they denied me entry and sent me back home.

But on the plane, God said to me, "You are *big*!" I was taken aback.

"How am I big when you could have destroyed their plans and let me in?"

The Lord said, "Look, you used to cast out demons only, but now entire territorial armies rage against you. Have you not read, 'Why do the nations rage, and the people plot a vain thing?'

The devil's strategy backfired. Not only was I made aware of my promotion in the Spirit, but I also strengthened our Miracle TV network in that country and improved our television channel quality. In the final analysis, we touched more people in that country than I ever would have had I been allowed to enter. Churches started growing exponentially, and to this day are still growing. The devil used the president as his strategy. I used TV as my strategy and yielded optimum results.

At one time, Paul rented a house and allowed people to visit him. He used that house as a training ground. That is the reason he said when you are in Rome, do what the Romans do: use strategic warfare (see 1 Corinthians 9:19-23). Again, in Galatians chapter 2, verse 2, Paul said I went to people of notable reputation so that I may not run in vain.

Galatians 2:2
And I went up by revelation, and communicated unto them that gospel which I preach among the Gentiles, but privately to them which were of reputation, lest by any means I should run, or had run, in vain.

The Amplified version says it this way:

Galatians 2:2 AMPC
I went because it was specially and divinely revealed to me that I should go, and I put before them the Gospel [declaring to them that] which I preach among the Gentiles. However, [I presented the matter] privately before those of repute, [for I wanted to make certain, by thus at first confining my communication to this private conference] that I was not running or had not run

in vain [guarding against being discredited either in what I was planning to do or had already done].

It was "specially and divinely revealed" to him what to do so that he could "[guard] against being discredited either in what [he] was planning to do or had already done." You see, it was a divine strategy.

The strength of a military campaign is in its strategy. Spiritual warfare does not happen accidentally. It is something that is strategically planned by the Military Commander, the Extraordinary Strategist. Just as any army plans its line of attack before a battle begins, the devil plans a line of attack and decides which methods he will use. It's a well-thought-out assault. But, he's no match for the Extraordinary Strategist.

The battle plan you need for warfare is not based on your own natural talent, mental capabilities, or human effort. Just as spiritual weapons come from God, so do spiritual strategies. The Holy Spirit always holds the key to every victory, and He wants to provide you with divinely-inspired strategies that will render the works of the devil null and void. If you will listen to the Holy Spirit, He will lead, move, and guide you, giving you strategies that will outwit the devil every time!

Lightning Source UK Ltd.
Milton Keynes UK
UKHW022335180320
360567UK00002B/3/J